Canaletto: 115 Masterpieces

By Maria Tsaneva

First Edition

*****

I0477252

<u>Canaletto: 115 Masterpieces</u>
*****

Foreword

Giovanni Antonio Canal (1697 – 1768) better known as
Canaletto, was an Italian painter of landscapes of
Venice. He was also an important printmaker in
etching.

He was born in Venice as the son of the painter
Bernardo Canal, hence his mononym Canaletto ("little
Canal"), and Artemisia Barbieri. Bernardo Bellotto was
his nephew and pupil. Canaletto served his
apprenticeship with his father and his brother. He
began in his father's occupation, that of a theatrical
scene painter. Canaletto was inspired by the Roman
vedutista Giovanni Paolo Pannini, and started painting
the daily life of the city and its people. After returning
from Rome in 1719, he began painting in his
topographical style. His first known signed and dated
work is Architectural Capriccio (1723). Studying with
the older Luca Carlevarijs, a moderately-talented
painter of urban cityscapes, he rapidly became his
master's equal.

Much of Canaletto's early artwork was painted "from nature", differing from the then customary practice of completing paintings in the studio. Some of his later works do revert to this custom, as suggested by the tendency for distant figures to be painted as blobs of colour – an effect produced by using a camera obscura, which blurs farther-away objects. However, his paintings are always notable for their accuracy: he recorded the seasonal submerging of Venice in water and ice. In this painting, the high viewpoint gives the illusion of looking out of a window, but there is no building in the position where the artist would have had to stand to use the "camera".

Canaletto's early works remain his most coveted and, according to many authorities, his best. One of his early pieces is The Stonemason's Yard (1729) which depicts a humble working area of the city.

Later Canaletto painted grand scenes of the canals of Venice and the Doge's Palace. His large-scale landscapes portrayed the city's pageantry and waning traditions, making innovative use of atmospheric effects and strong local colors. For these qualities, his works may be said to have anticipated Impressionism.

Many of his pictures were sold to Englishmen on their Grand Tour, often through the agency of the merchant Joseph Smith, who was later appointed British Consul in Venice in 1744. It was Smith who acted as an agent for Canaletto, first in requesting paintings of Venice from the painter in the early 1720s and helping him to sell his paintings to other Englishmen.

In the 1740s Canaletto's market was disrupted when the War of the Austrian Succession led to a reduction in the number of British visitors to Venice. Smith also arranged for the publication of a series of etchings of "capricci" (or architectural phantasies) in his vedute ideale, but the returns were not high enough, and in 1746 Canaletto moved to London, to be closer to his market. He remained in England until 1755, producing views of London (including the Westminster Bridge) and of his patrons' castles and houses. His 1754 painting of Old Walton Bridge includes an image of Canaletto himself. He was often expected to paint England in the fashion with which he had painted his native city. Canaletto's painting began to suffer from repetitiveness, losing its fluidity, and becoming mechanical. The artist was compelled to give public painting demonstrations in order to refute this claim; however, his reputation never fully recovered in his lifetime.

After his return to Venice, Canaletto was elected to the Venetian Academy in 1763. He continued to paint until his death in 1768. In his later years he often worked from old sketches, but he sometimes produced surprising new compositions. He was willing to make subtle alternations to topography for artistic effect.

His pupils included his nephew Bernardo Bellotto, Francesco Guardi, Michele Marieschi, Gabriele Bella, and Giuseppe Moretti. The painter, Giuseppe Bernardino Bison was a follower of his style. Canaletto's views always fetched high prices, and as early as the 18th century Catherine the Great and other European monarchs vied for his grandest paintings.

Paintings

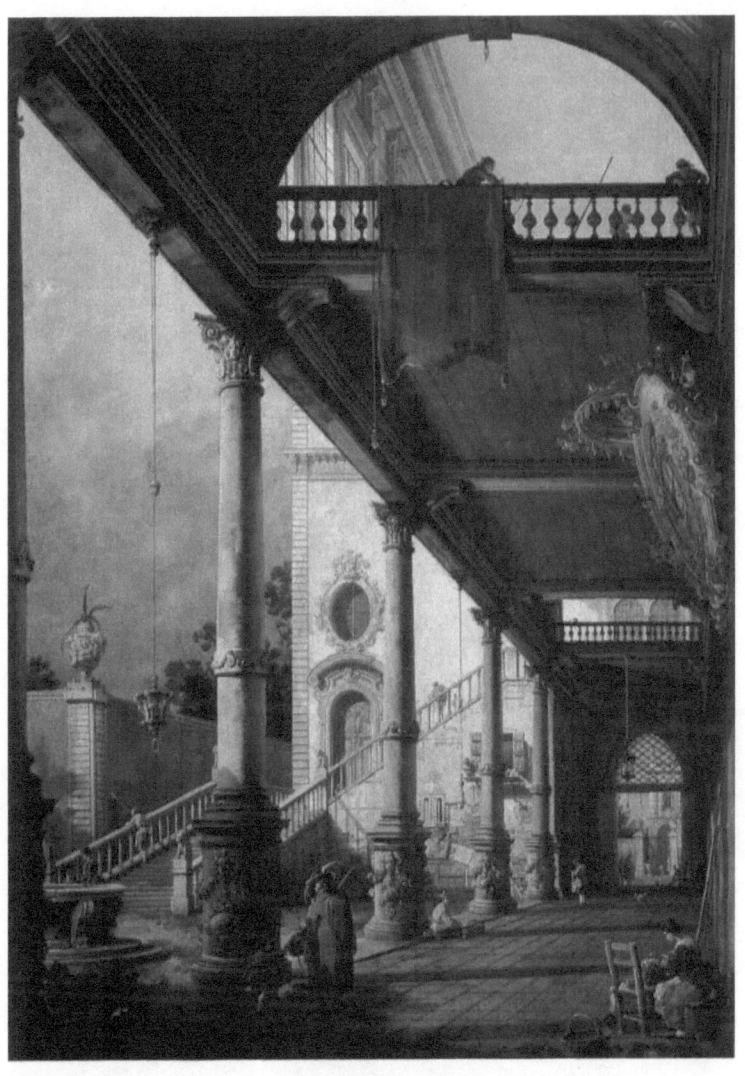

Architectural
Oil on canvas

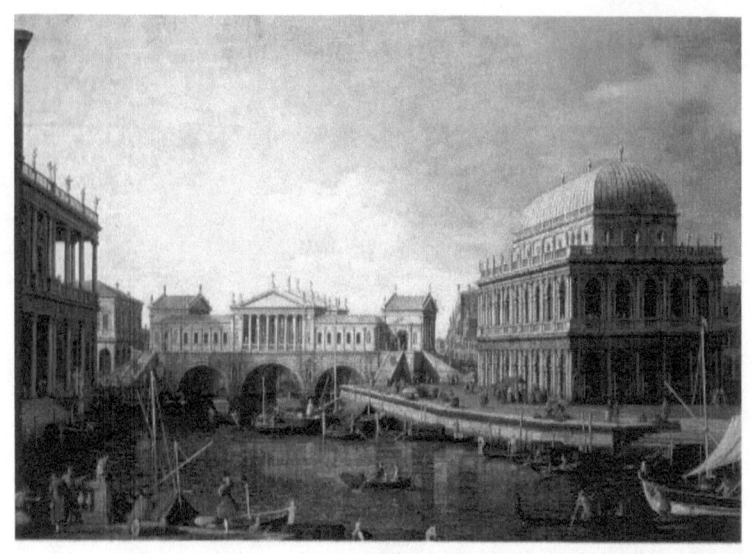

Basilica di Vecenza and the Ponte de Rialto
Oil on canvas

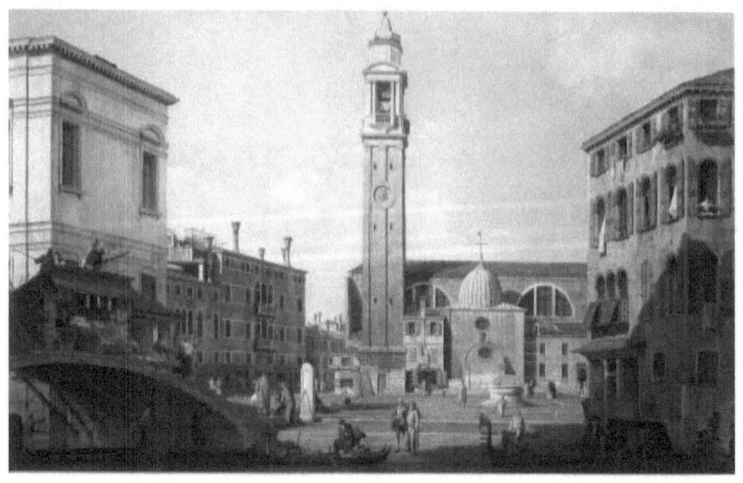

Camo Santi Apostoli
Oil on canvas

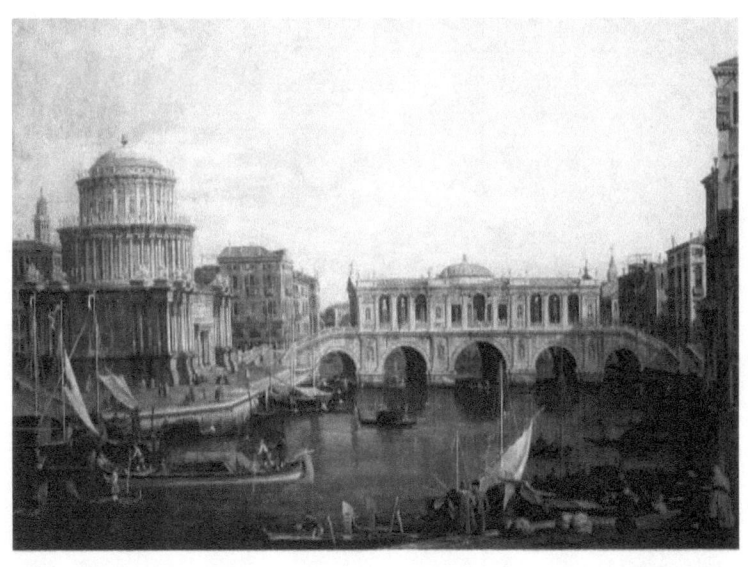

Capriccio of the Grand Canal with an Imaginary Rialto
Bridge and Other Buildings
Oil on canvas

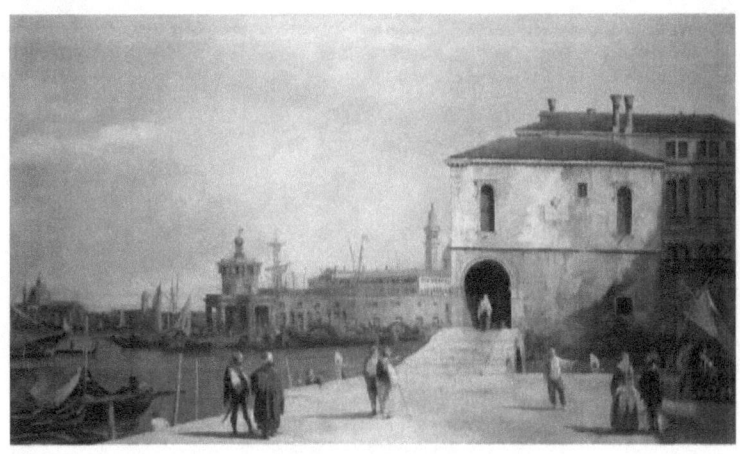

Fonteghetto della Farina
Oil on canvas

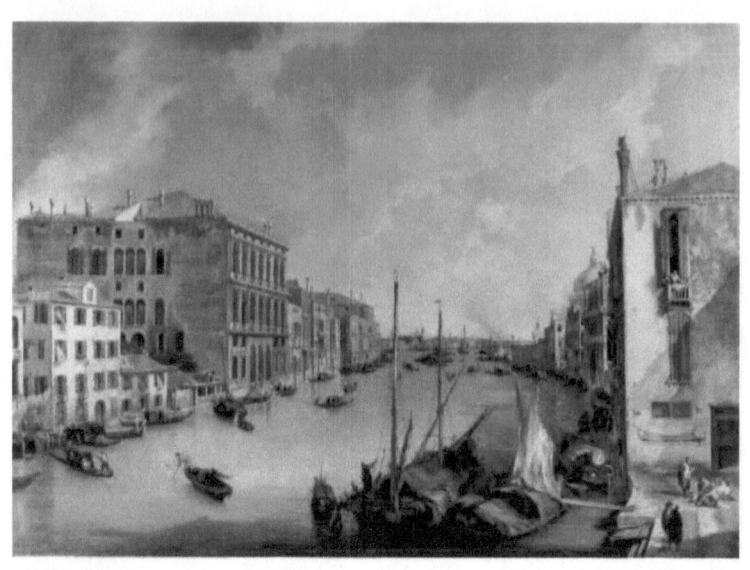

Grand Canal: Looking East from the Campo S. Vio
Oil on canvas

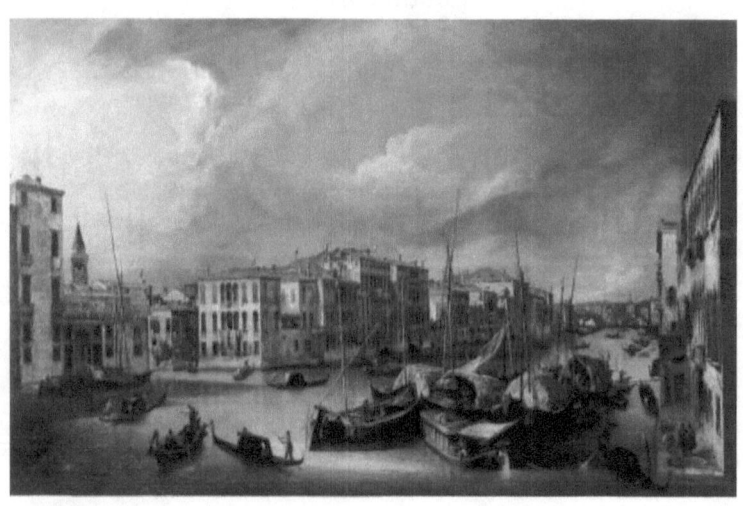

Grand Canal: Looking Northeast from near the Palazzo
Corner Spinelli to the Rialto Bridge
Oil on canvas

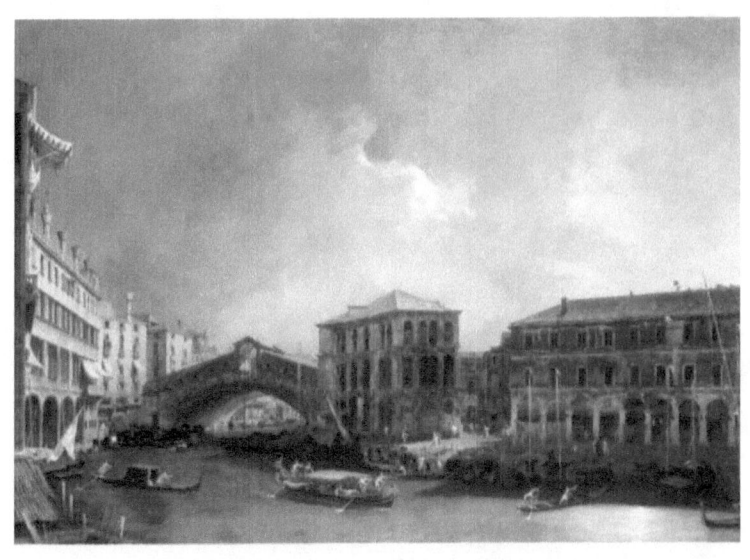

Grand Canal: the Rialto Bridge from the North
Oil on canvas

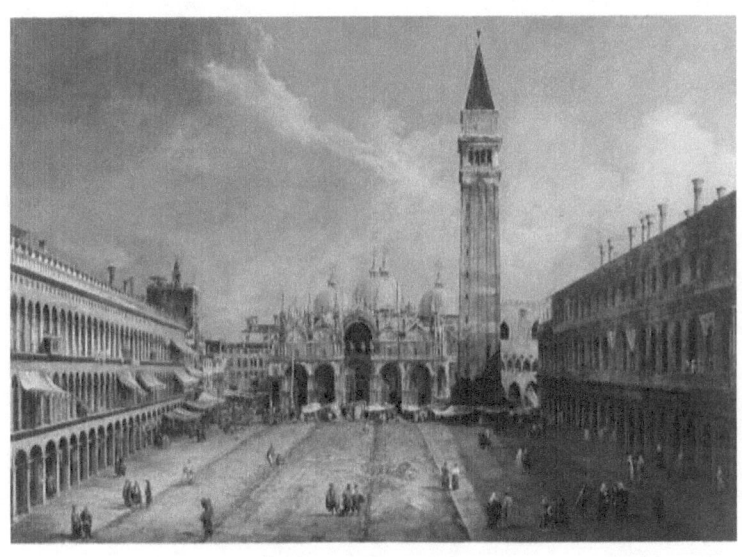

The Piazza San Marco in Venice, 1724
Oil on canvas

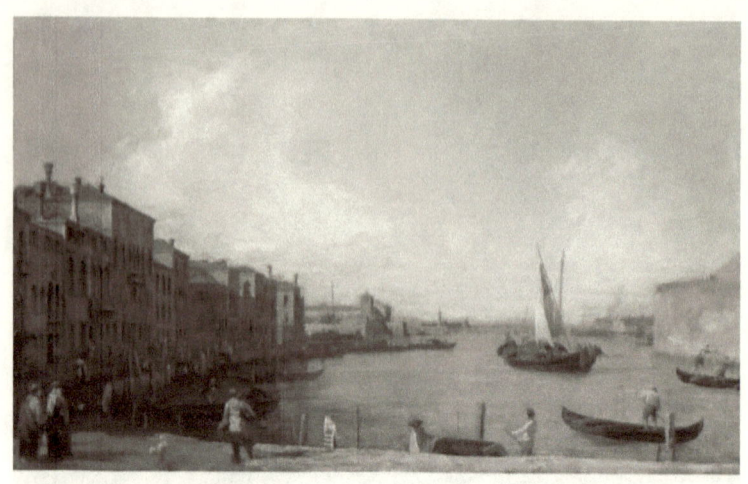

Venice: The Canale di S. Chiari towards the Lagoon, 1724, Oil on canvas

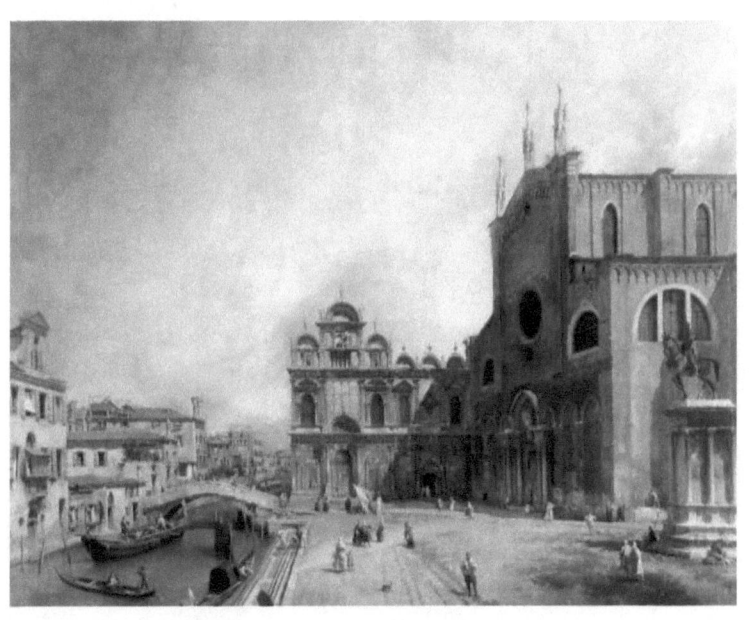

SS. Giovanni e Paulo and the Scuola de San Marco, 1725
Oil on canvas

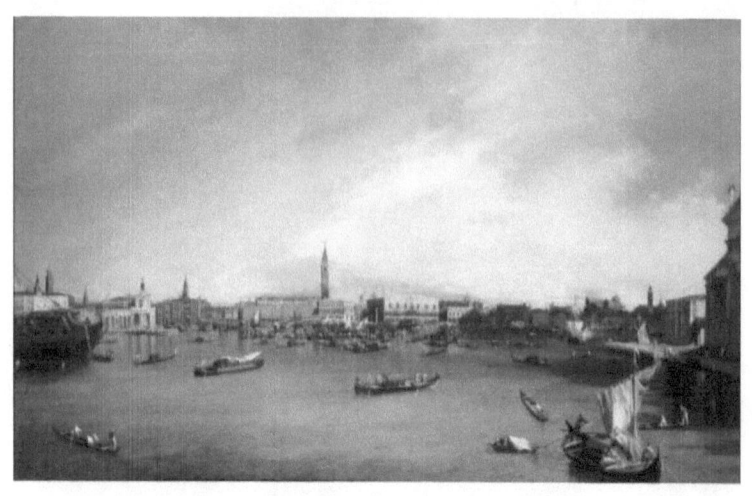

The Bacino di San Marco, Venice, Seen from the
Giudecca, 1726
Oil on canvas

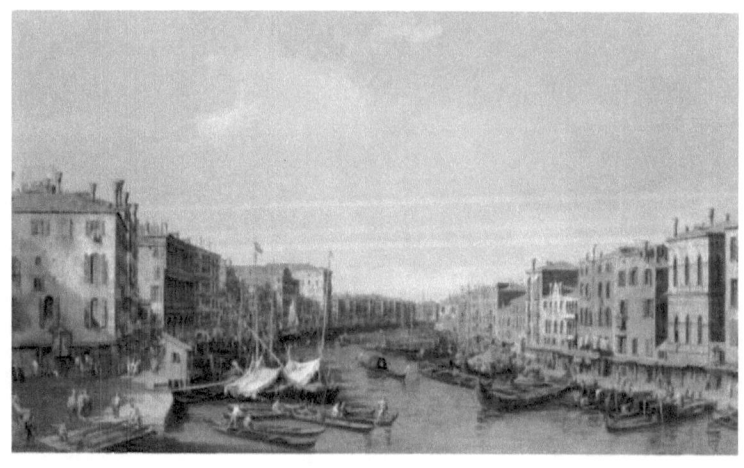

Venice: The Grand Canal from the Rialto to the Palazzo
Foscari, 1726
Oil on canvas

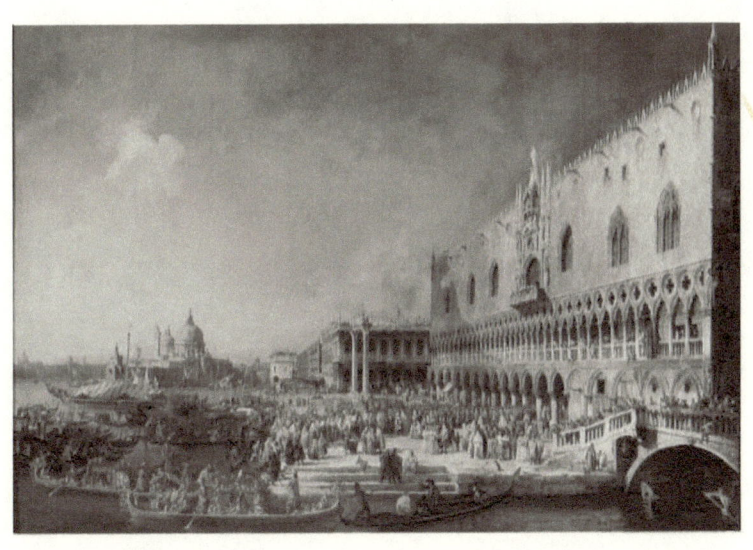

The Reception of the French Ambassador Jacques-
Vincent Languet, Compte de Gergy, at the Doge's
Palace, 1726
Oil on canvas

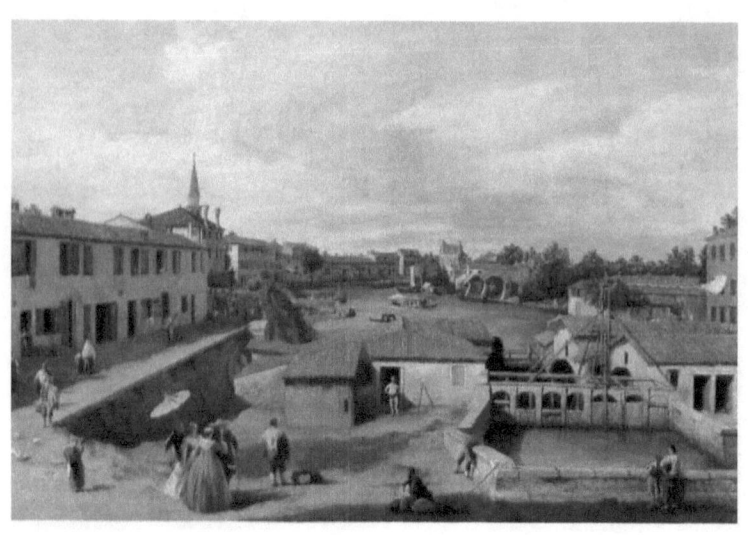

Sluice Gates at Dolo, 1727
Oil on canvas

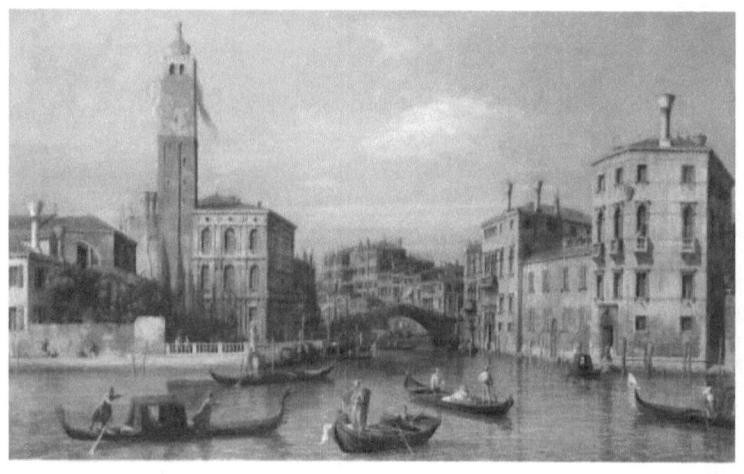

Venice: S. Geremia and the Entrance to the Cannaregio,
1727, Oil on canvas

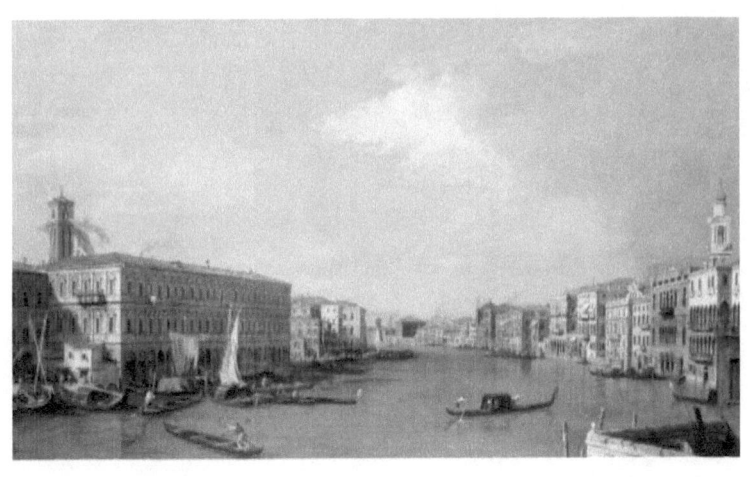

Venice: The Grand Canal Looking North from the
Rialto, 1727
Oil on canvas

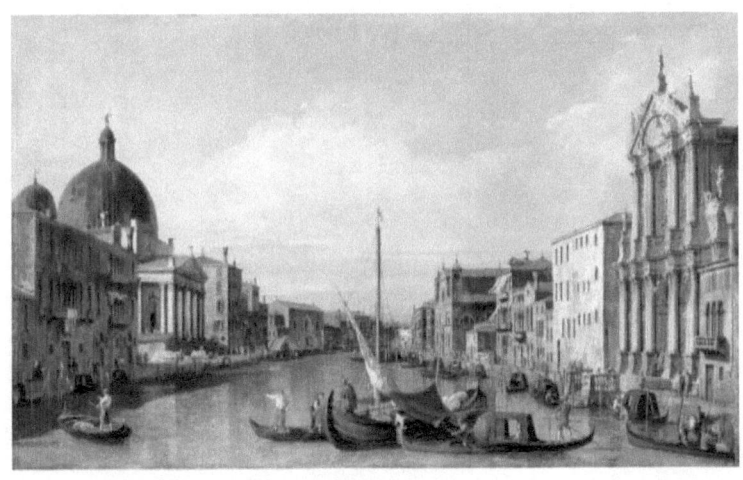

Venice: The Grand Canal with the Scalzi and S. Simione
Piccoli, 1727
Oil on canvas

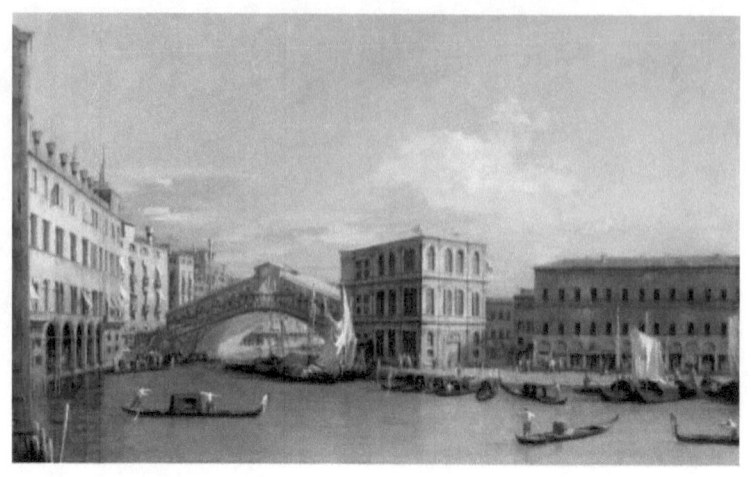

Venice: The Rialto Bridge from the North, 1727
Oil on canvas

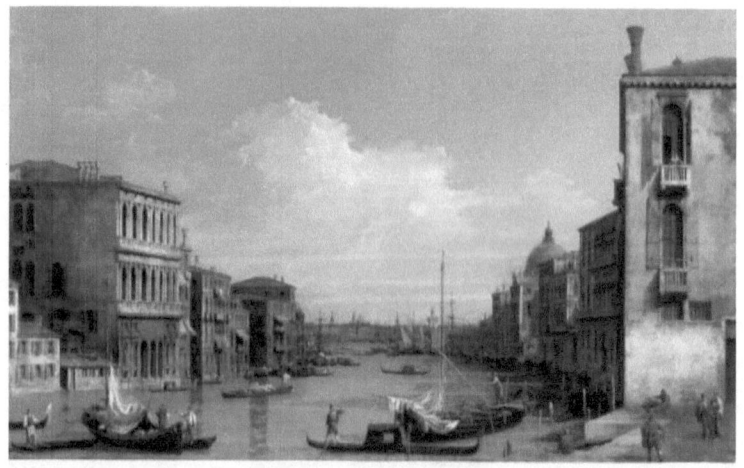

Venice: The Grand Canal from Campo S. Vio Towards
the Bacino, 1728
Oil on canvas

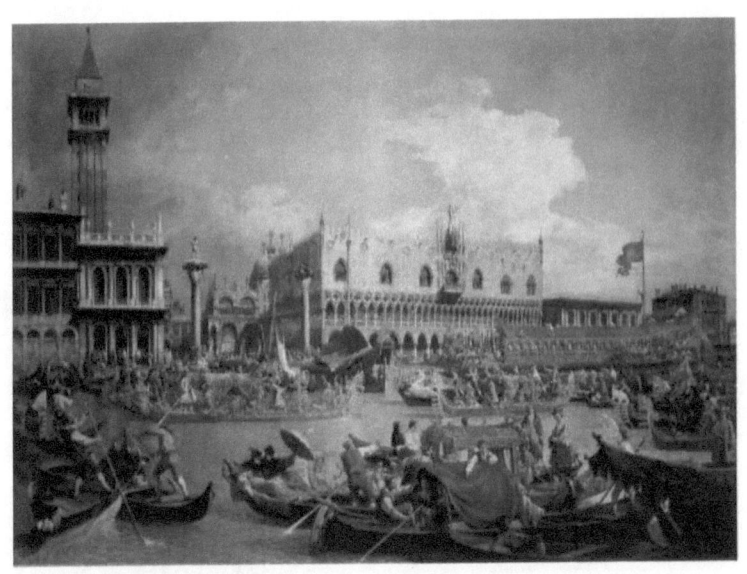

The Bucintgoro by the Molo on Ascension Day, 1729
Oil on canvas

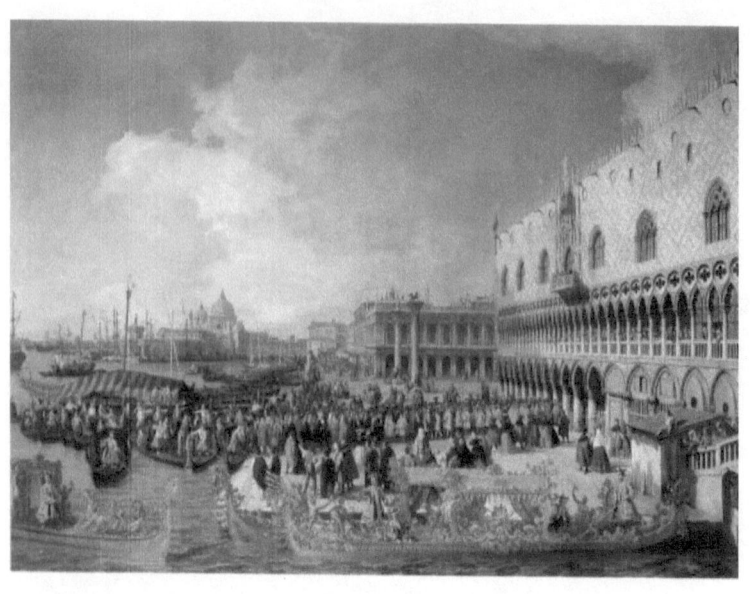

Reception of the Imperial Ambassador at the Doge's
Palace, 1729
Oil on canvas

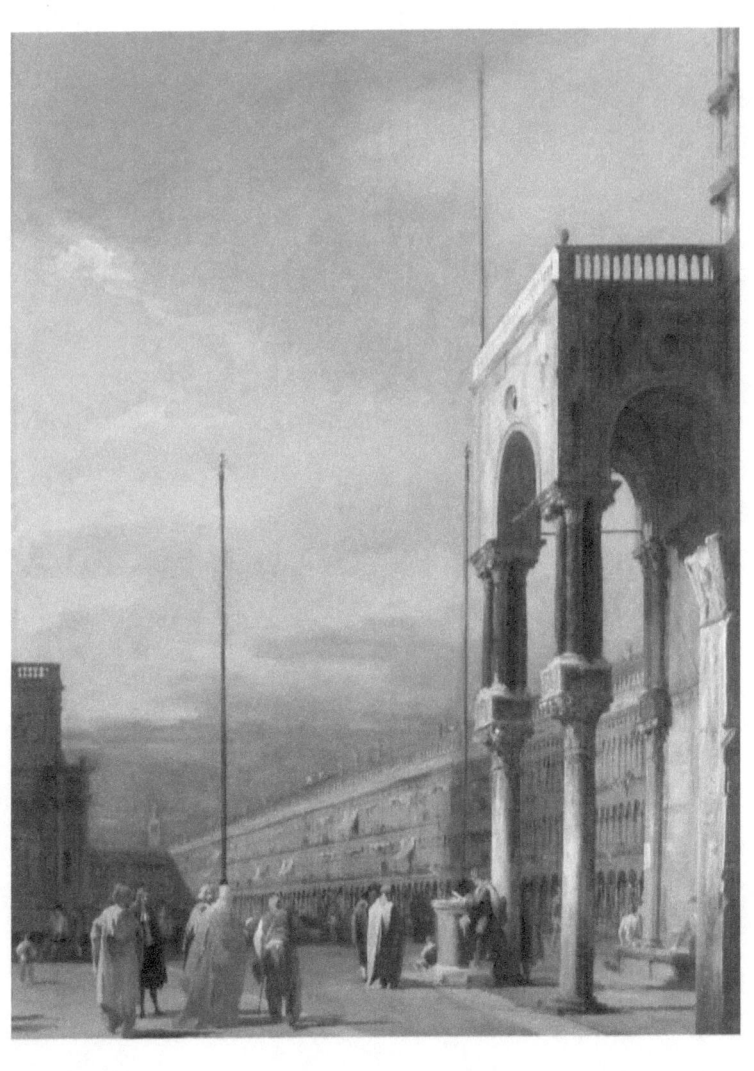

Venice: Piazza San Marco from a Corner of the Basilica,
1729
Oil on canvas

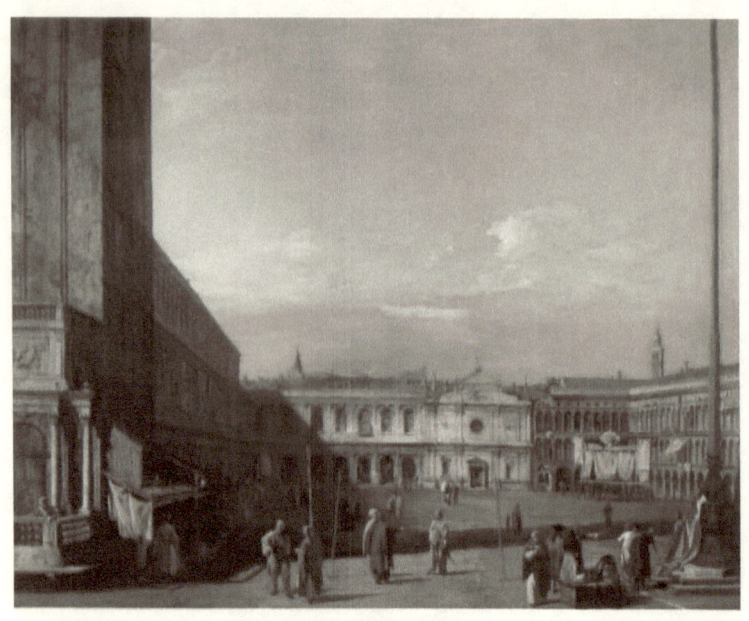

Venice: Piazza San Marco towards S. Geminiano, 1729
Oil on canvas

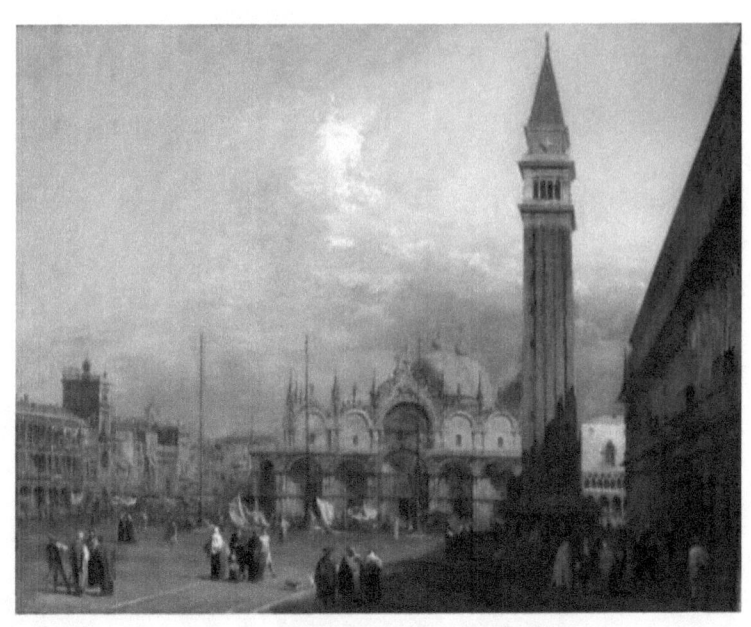

Venice: Piazza San Marco with the Basilica and
Campanile, 1729
Oil on canvas

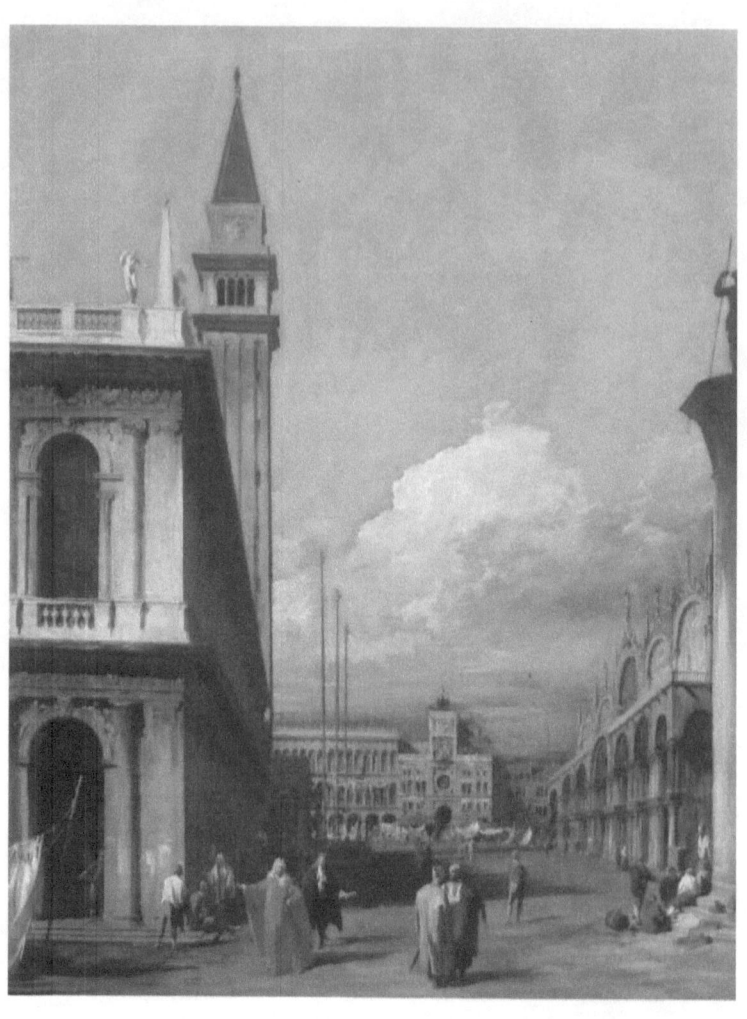

Venice: The Piazzetta towards the Torre dell Olorogio,
1729
Oil on canvas

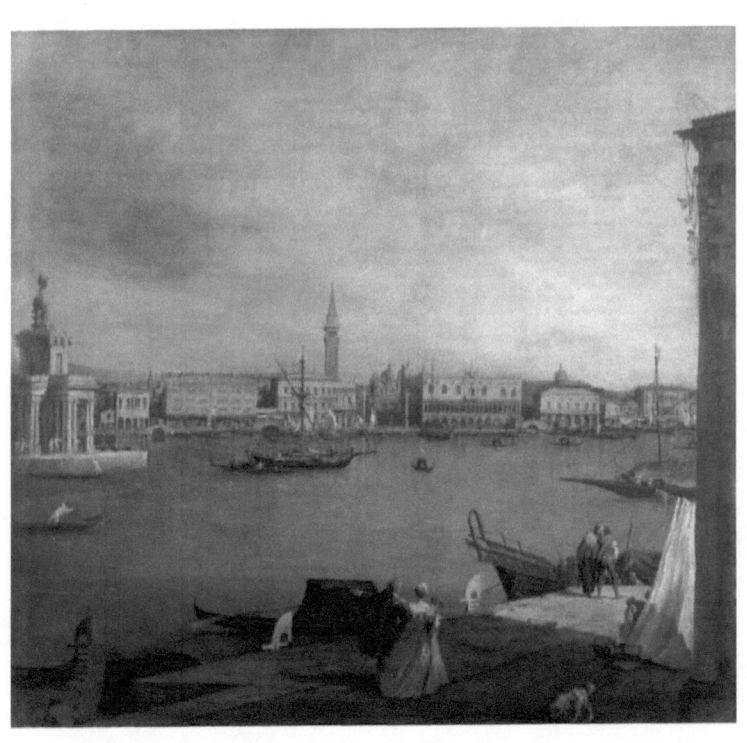

The Bacino di San Marco: Looking North, 1730
Oil on canvas

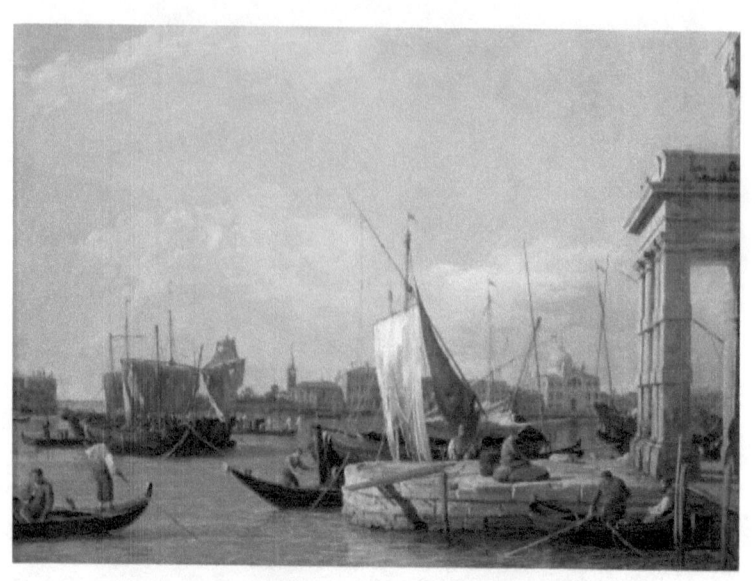

The Dogana in Venice, 1730
Oil on canvas

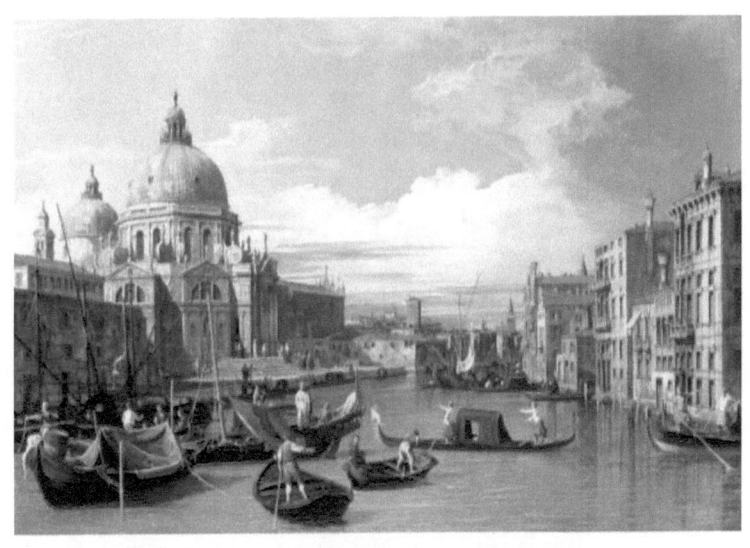

The Grand Canal and the Church Santa Maria della
Salute, 1730, Oil on canvas

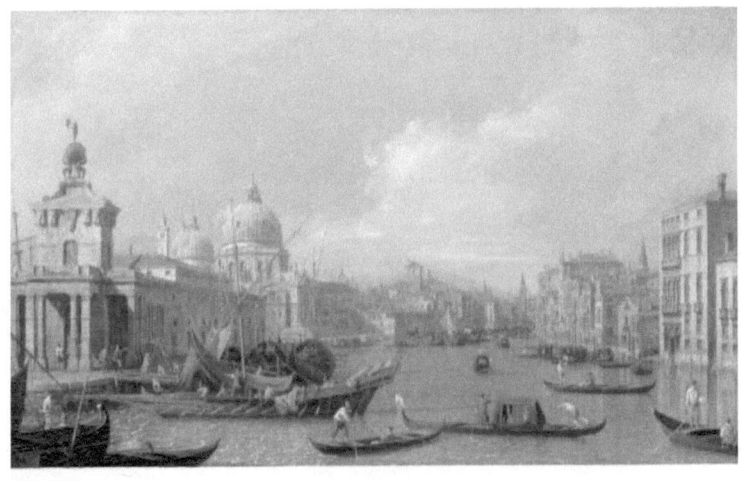

The Grand Canal from the Salute towards the Carita,
1730, Oil on canvas

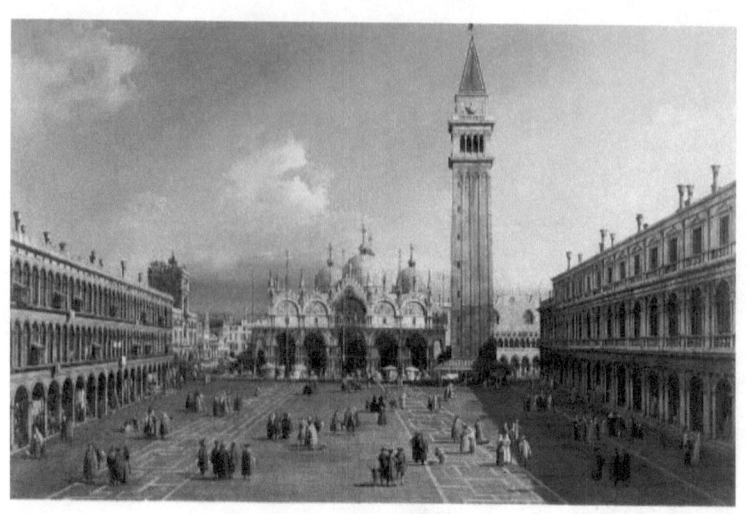

Piazza San Marco with the Basilica, 1730
Oil on canvas

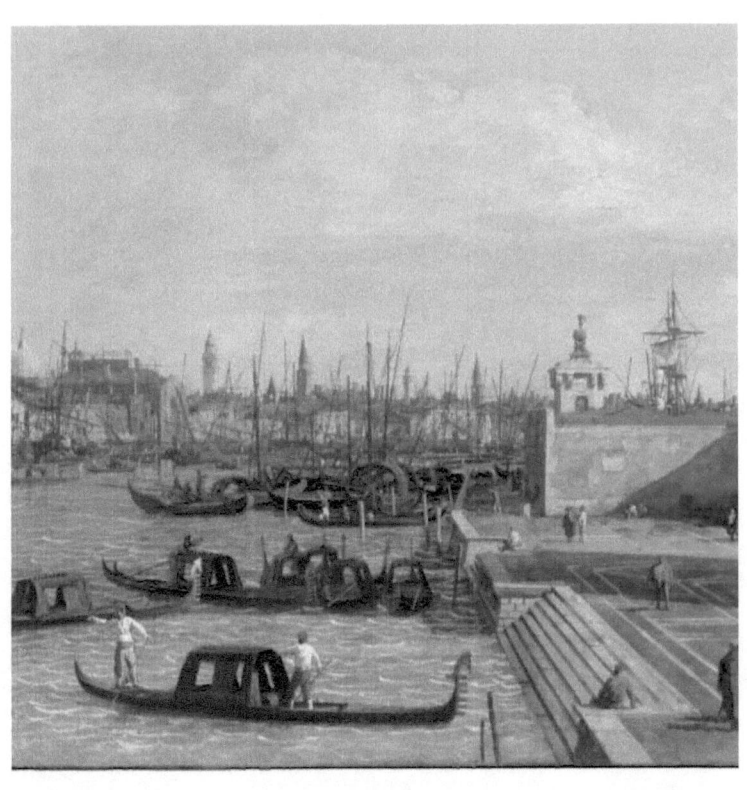

Venice: The Grand Canal with S. Maria della Salute
Towards the Riva degli Schiavoni, 1730
Oil on canvas

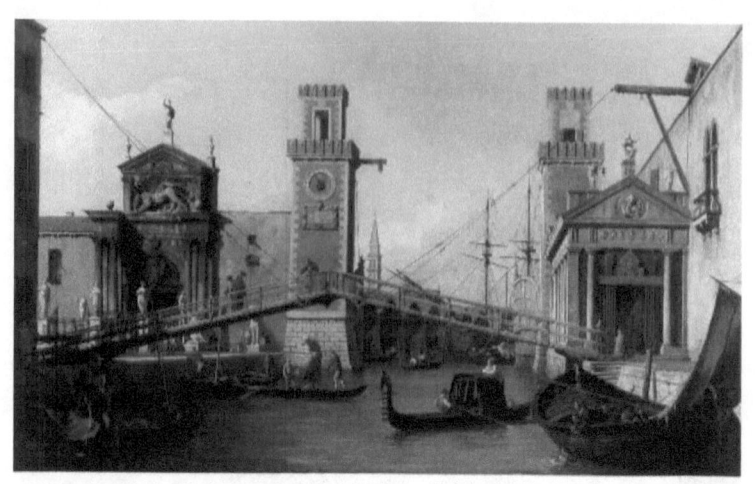

Entrance to the Arsenal, 1732
Oil on canvas

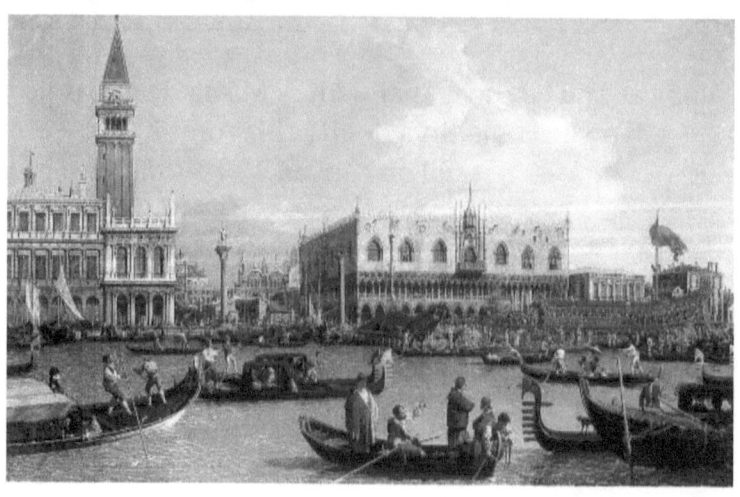

Return of the Bucentoro to the Molo on Ascension Day,
1732, Oil on canvas

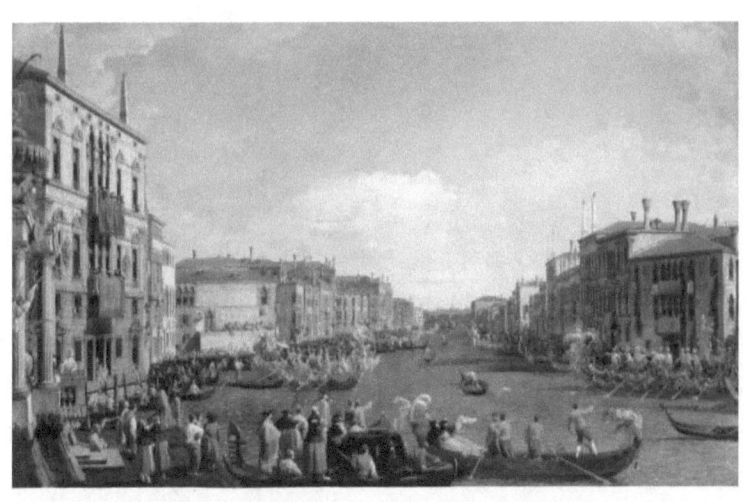

Venice: A Regatta on the Grand Canal, 1734
Oil on canvas

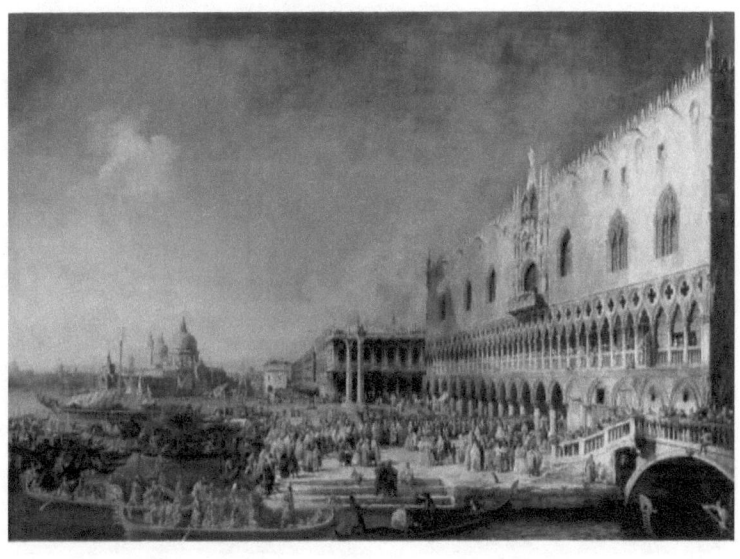

Arrival of the French Ambassador at the Doge's Palace,
1735, Oil on canvas

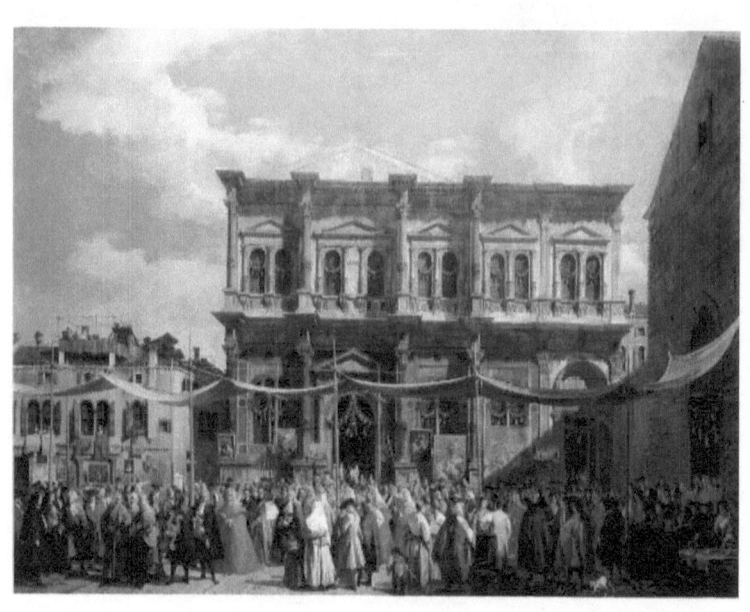

Feast Day of San Rocco, 1735
Oil on canvas

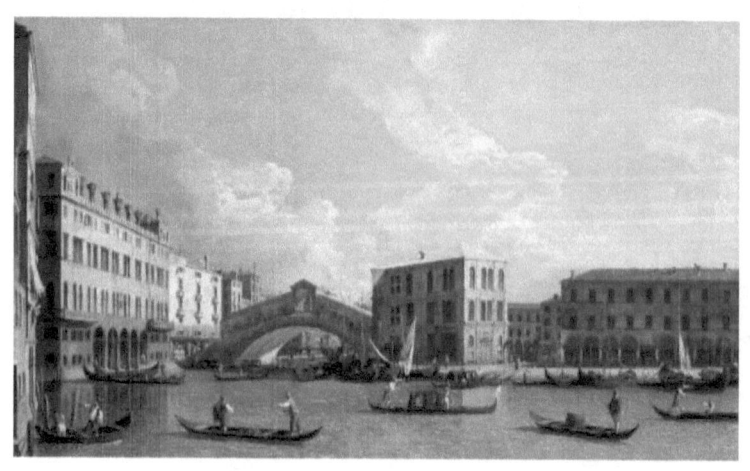

A View of the Rialto, Venice, 1735
Oil on canvas

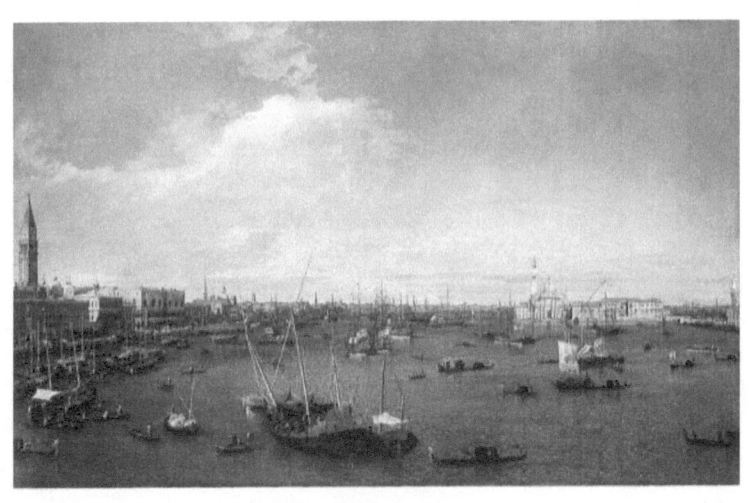

Bacino di San Marco, 1738
Oil on canvas

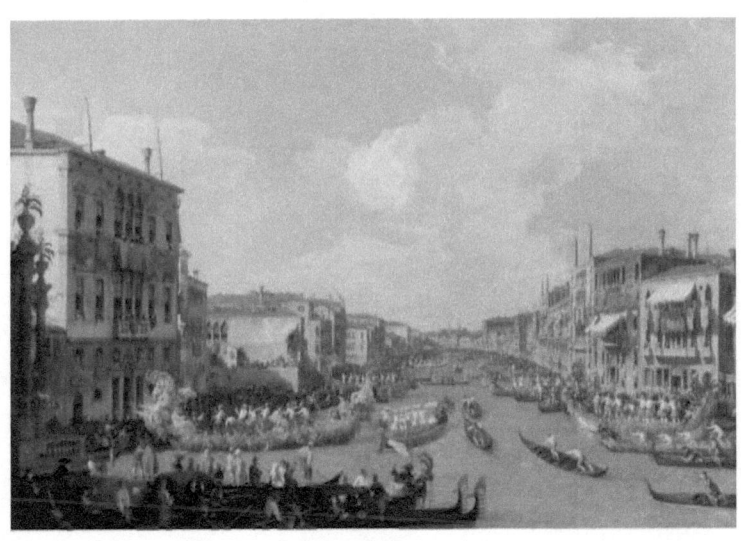

Regatta on the Grand Canal, Venice, Italy, 1739
Oil on canvas

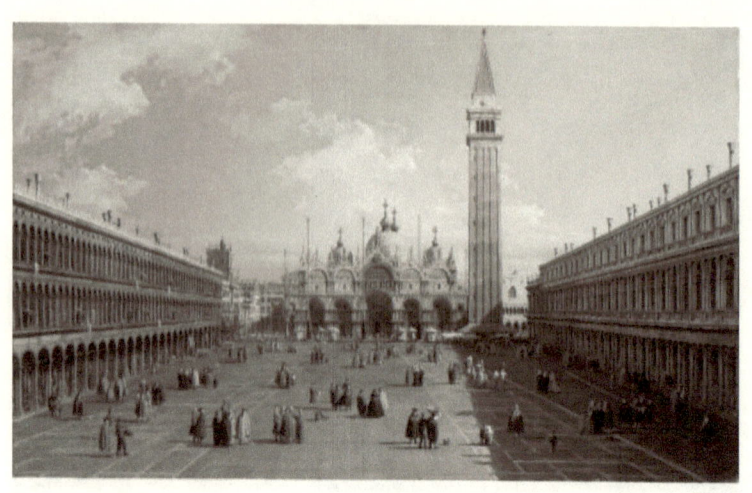

Venice, a View of Piazza San Marco Looking East
towards the Basilica, 1739
Oil on canvas

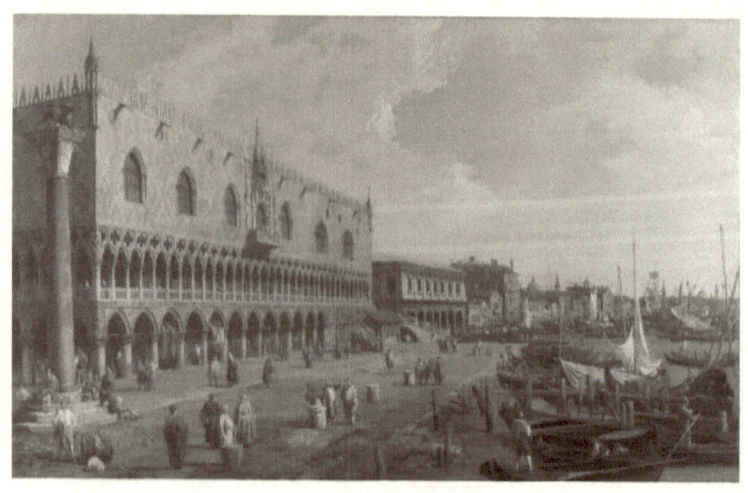

Venice: The Doge's Palace and the Riva degli Schiavoni,
1739, Oil on canvas

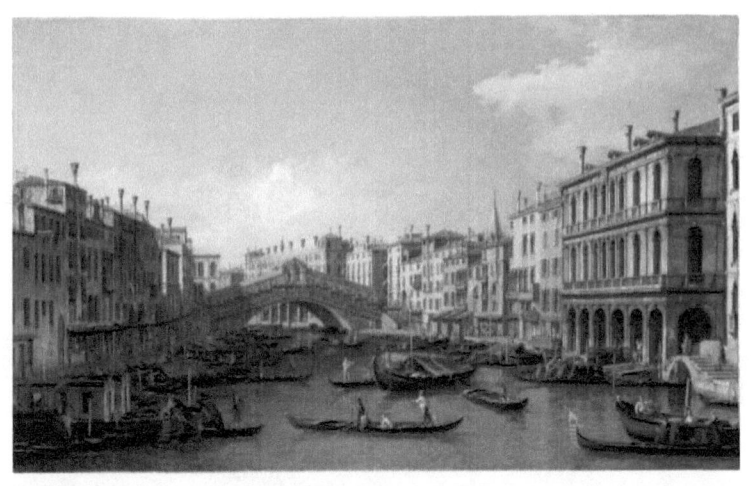

Venice, the Grand Canal Looking North-East from the
Palazzo Dolphin-Manin to the Rialto Bridge, 1739
Oil on canvas

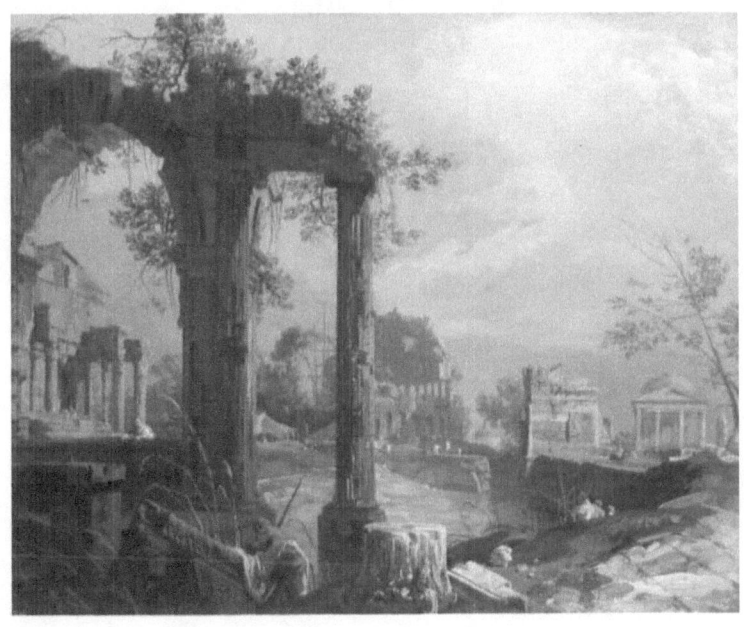

A Caprice: View with Ruins, 1740, Oil on canvas

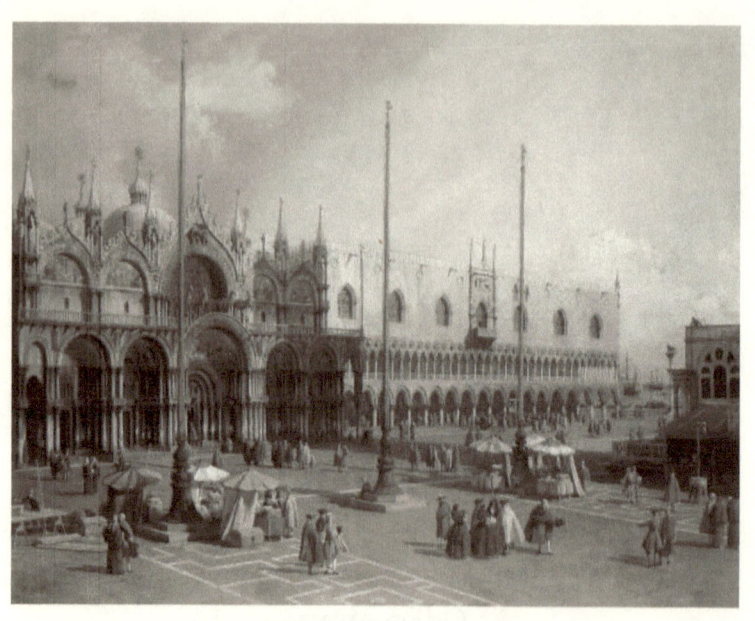

Piazza San Marco, 1740
Oil on canvas

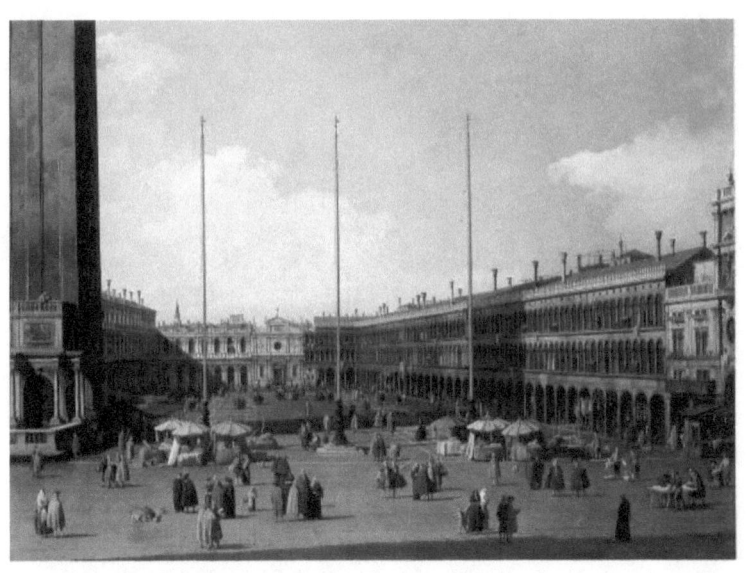

Piazza San Marco, Looking Towards San Geminiano, 1740, Oil on canvas

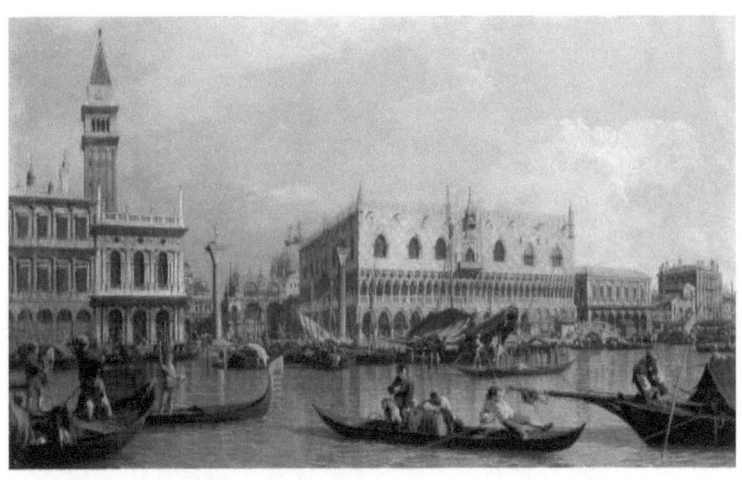

Piazzetta and the Doge's Palace from the Bacino di San Marco, 1740, Oil on canvas

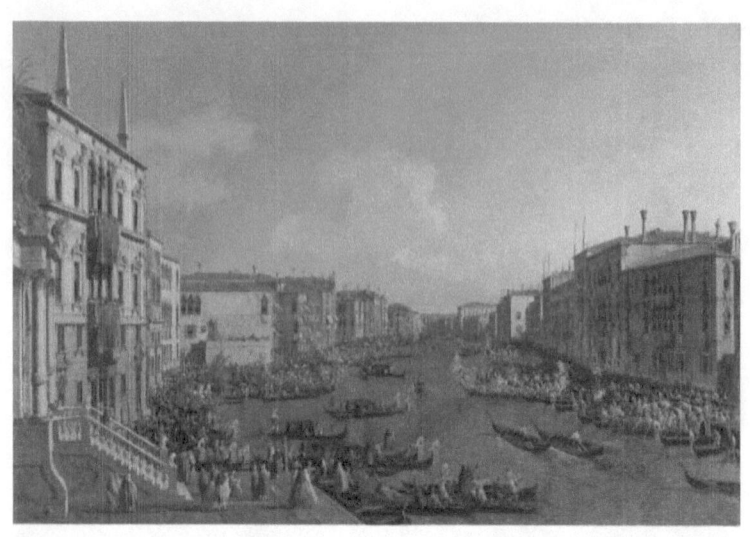

A Regatta on the Grand Canal, 1740
Oil on canvas

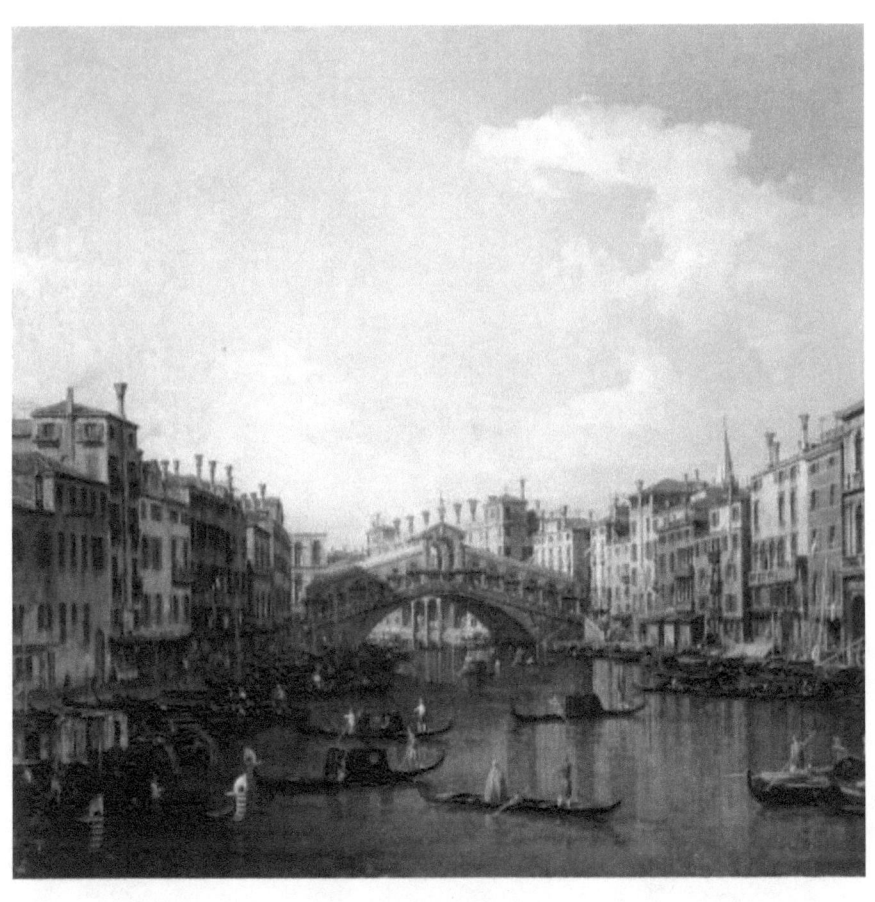

Rialto Bridge from the South, 1740
Oil on canvas

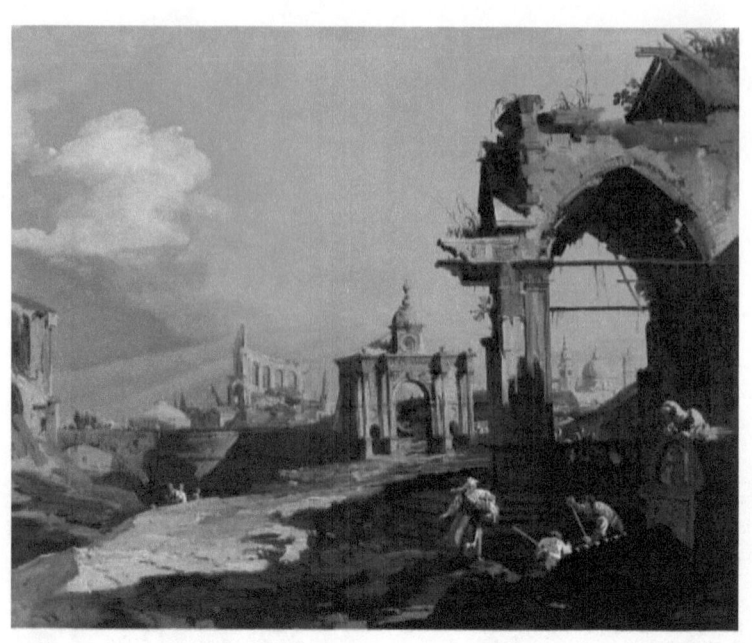

Venice: A Caprice View with a Pointed Arch, 1740
Oil on canvas

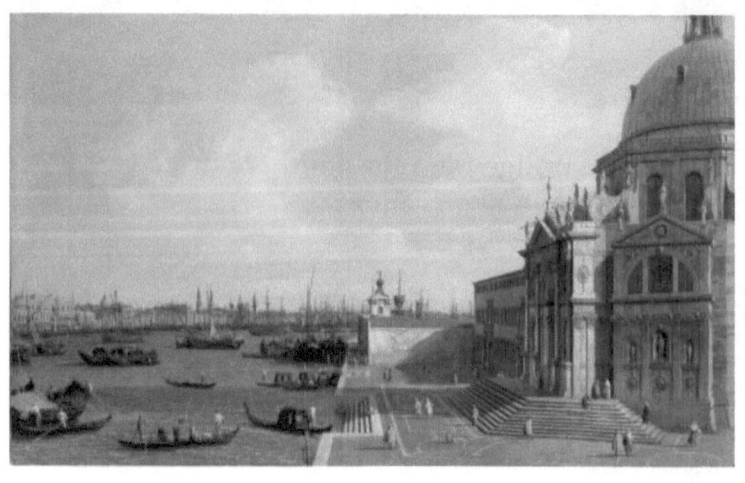

Venice, Santa Maria della Salute, 1740
Oil on canvas

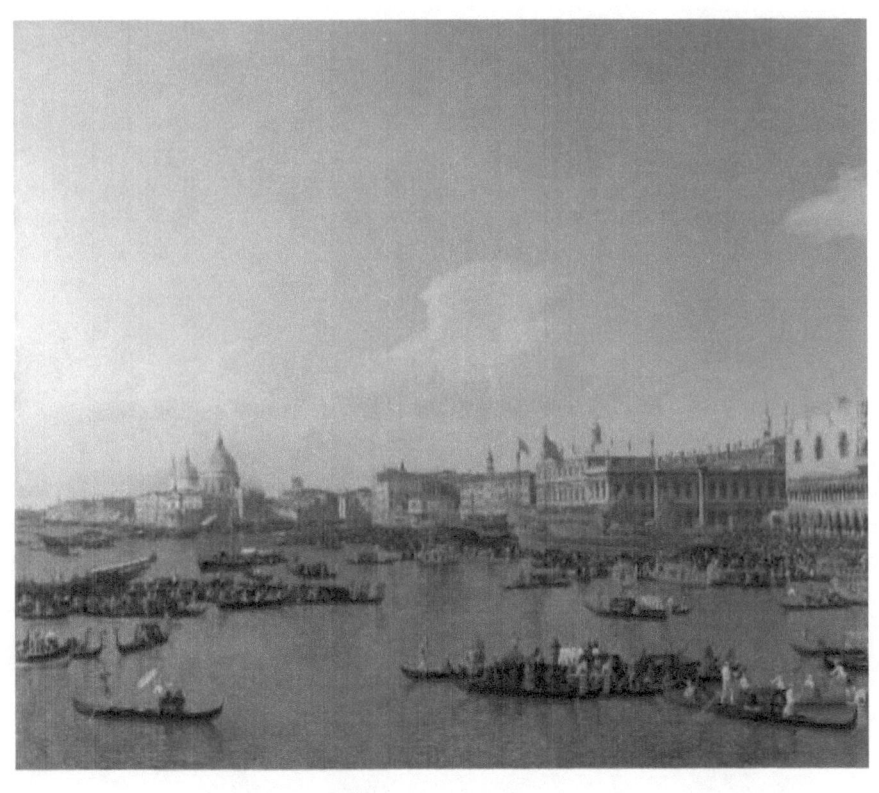

Venice: The Basin of San Marco on Ascension Day, 1740
Oil on canvas

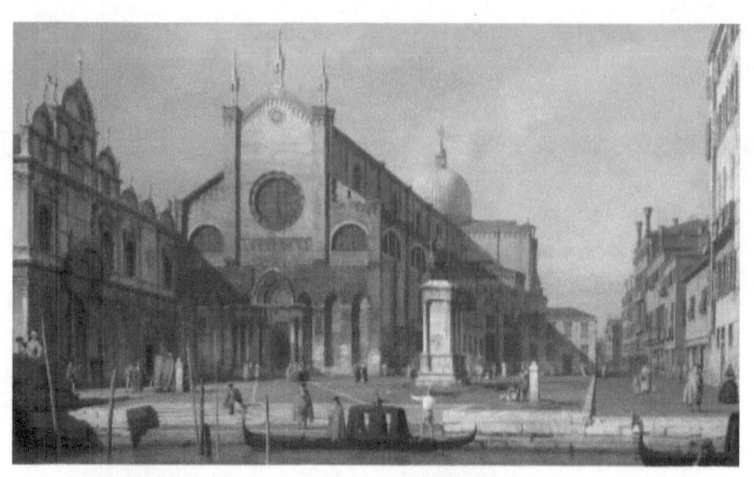

Venice: The Campo SS. Giovanni e Paolo, 1740
Oil on canvas

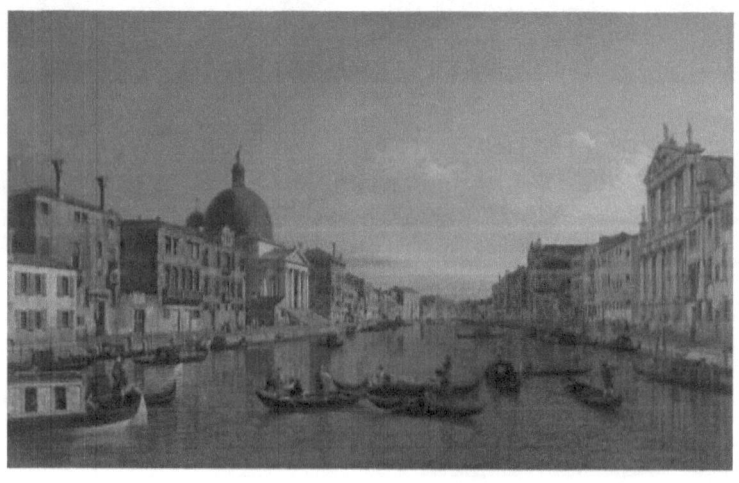

Venice: The Upper Reaches of the Grand Canal with S.
Simeone Piccolo, 1740, Oil on canvas

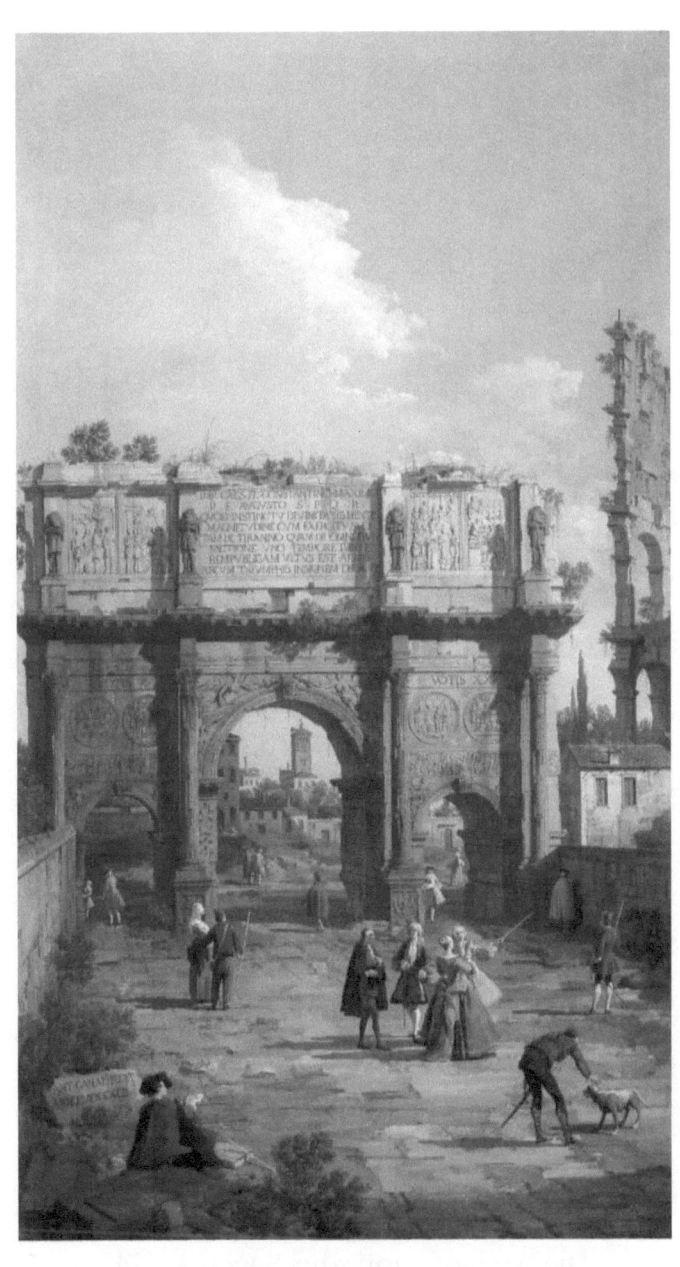

Arch of Constantine, 1742
Oil on canvas

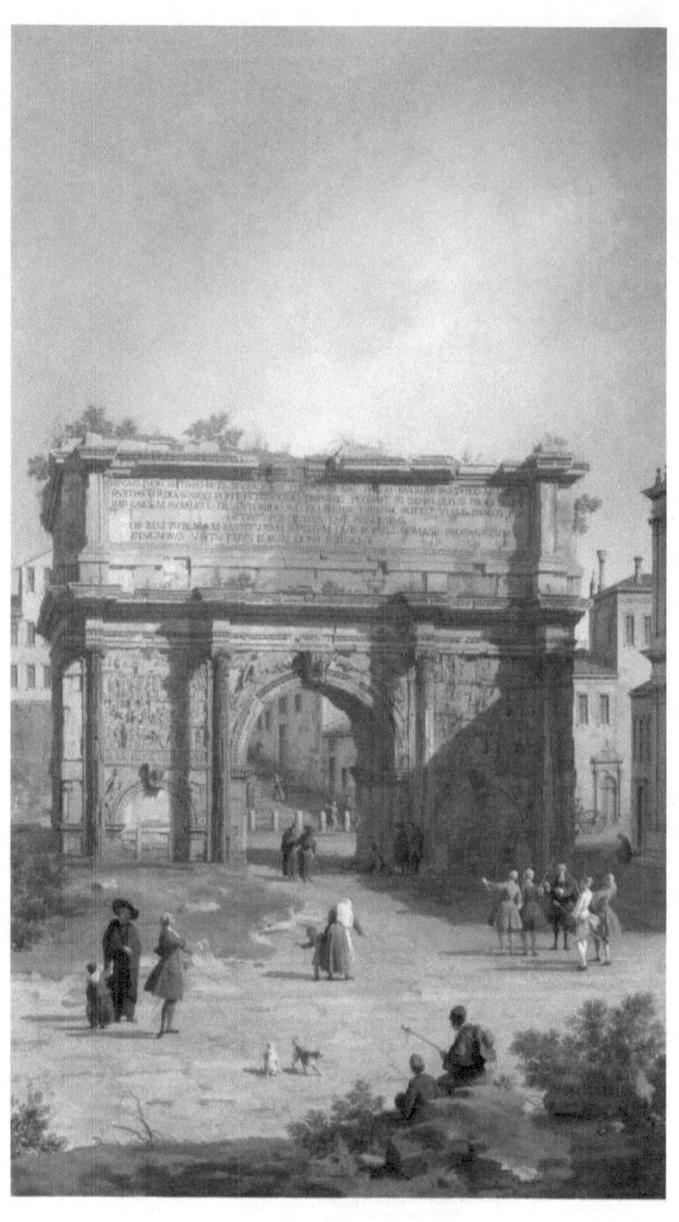

The Arch of Septimius Severus, 1742
Oil on canvas

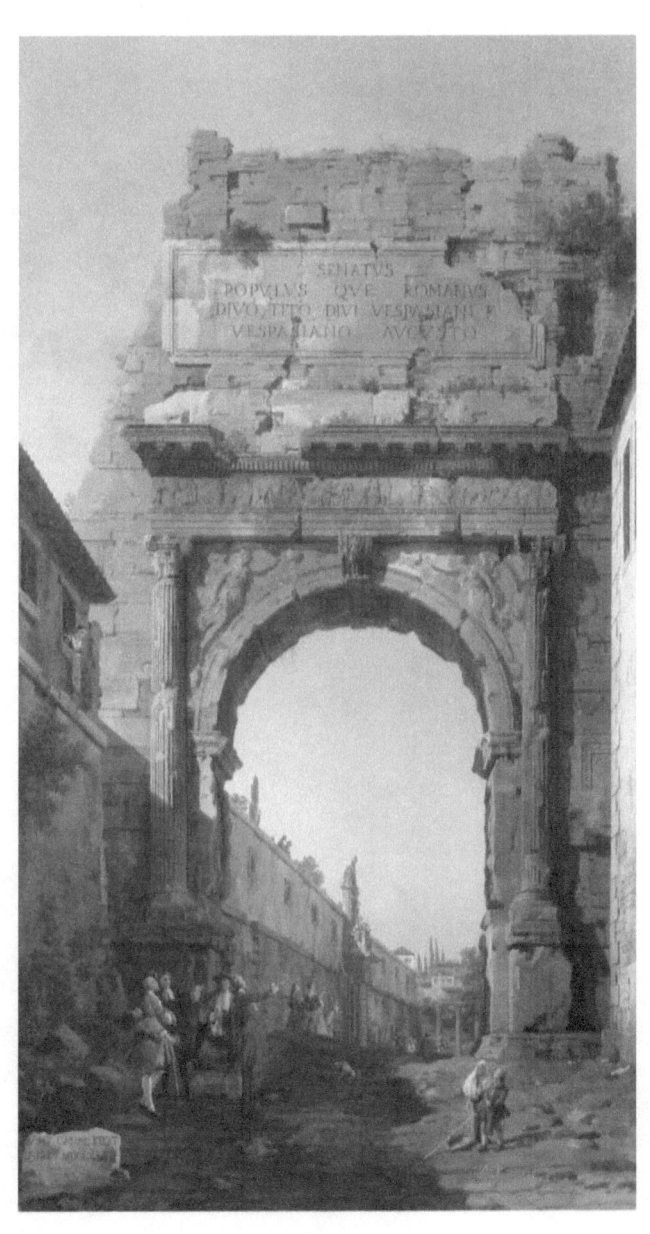

Arch of Titus, 1742
Oil on canvas

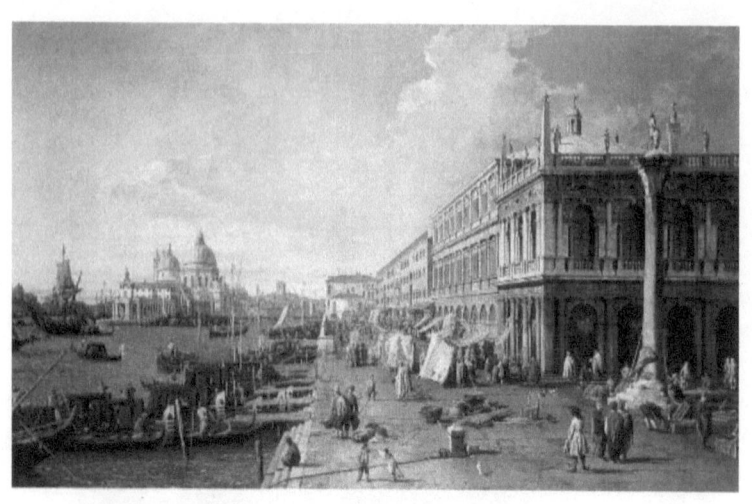

Molo with the Library, 1742
Oil on canvas

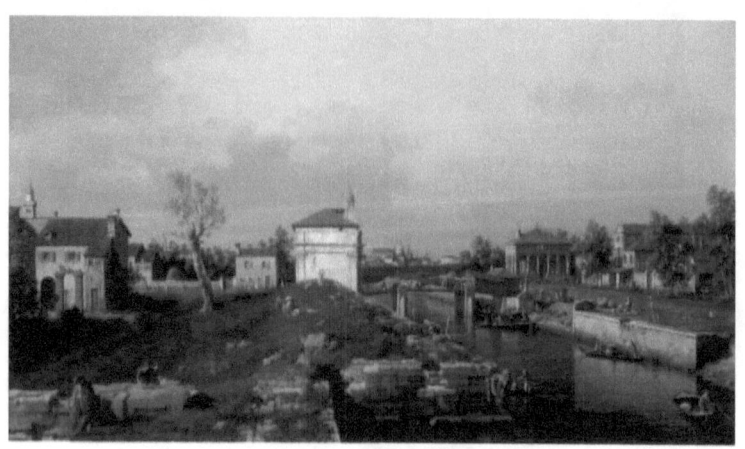

Porta Portello, Padua, 1742
Oil on canvas

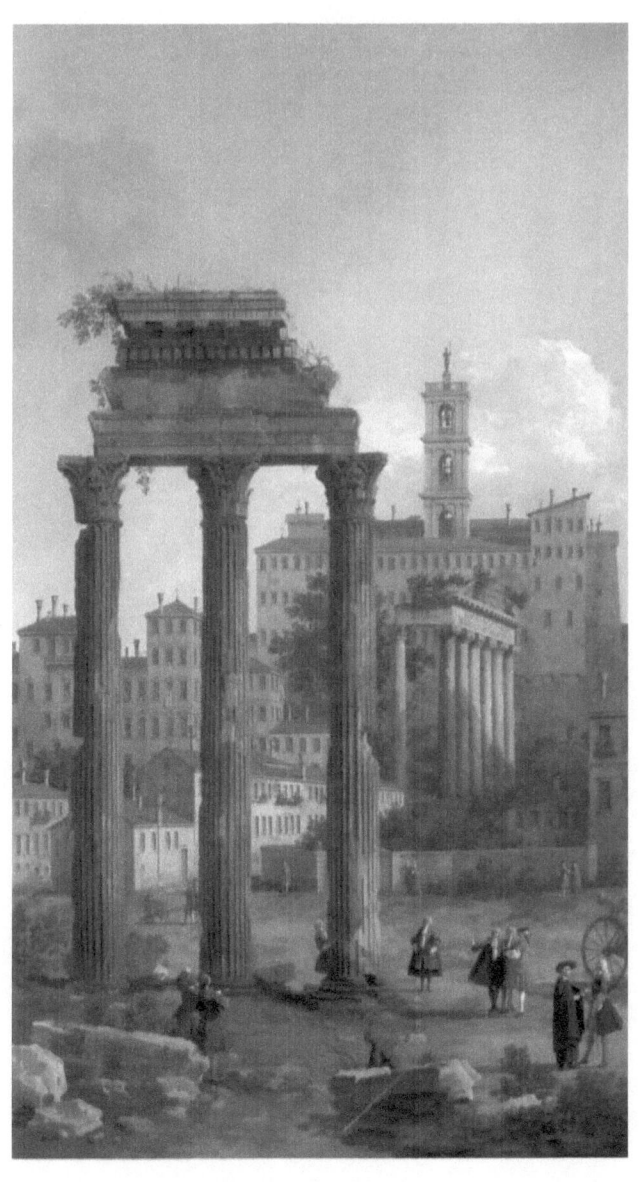

Rome: Ruins of the Forum looking Towards the Capitol, 1742, Oil on canvas

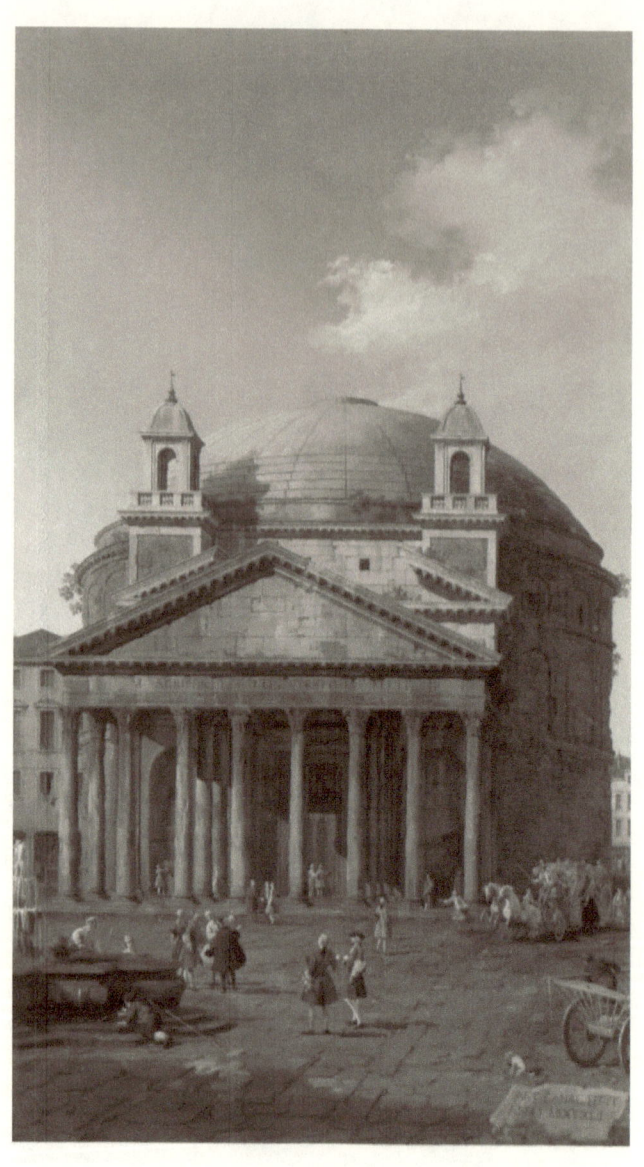

Rome: The Pantheon, 1742
Oil on canvas

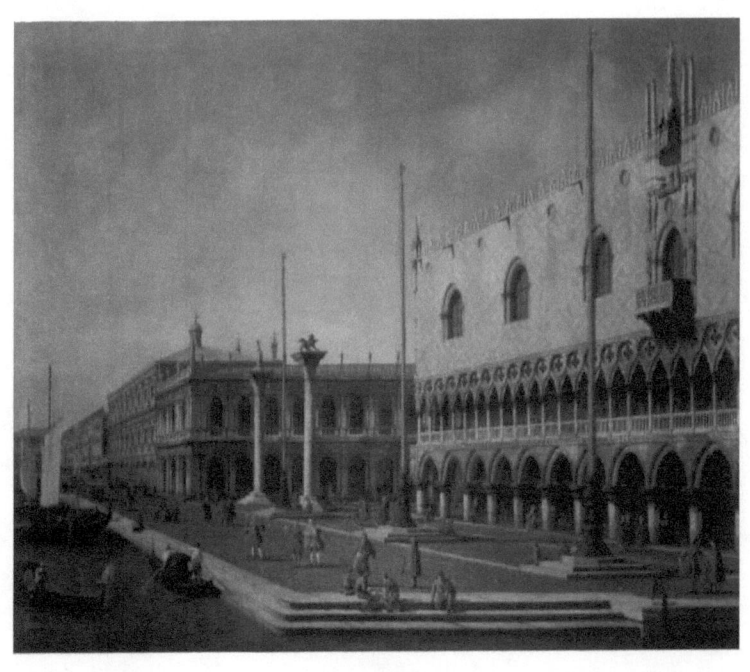

Caprice View of the Molo and the Doge's Palace, 1743
Oil on canvas

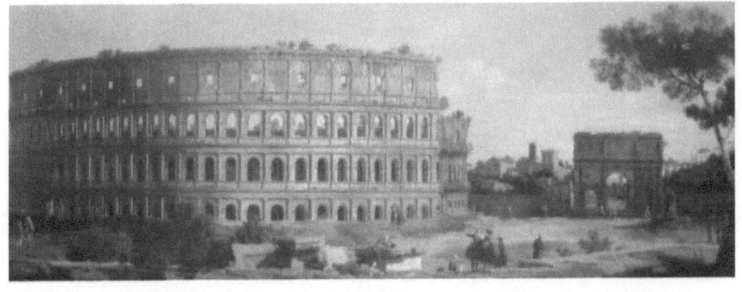

Rome: View of the Colosseum and the Arch of
Constantine, 1743, Oil on canvas

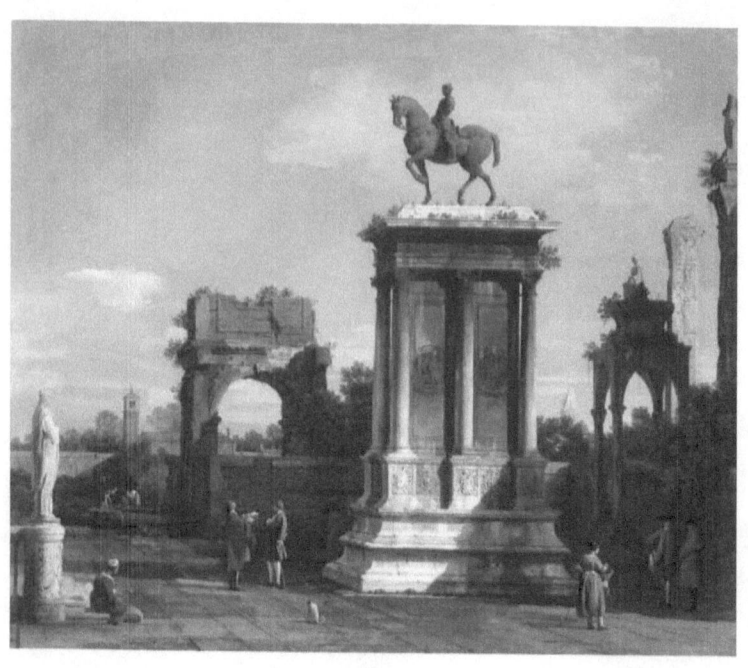

The Colleoni Monument in a Caprice Setting, 1744
Oil on canvas

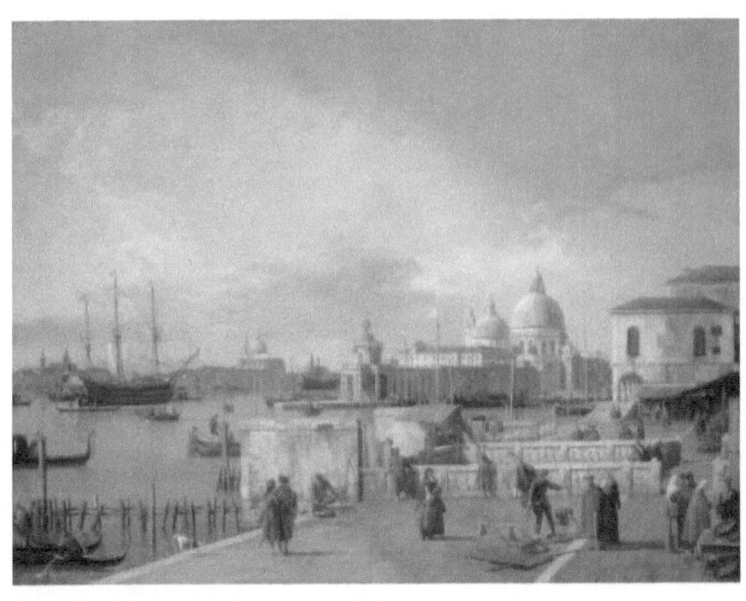

Entrance to the Grand Canal from the Molo, Venice,
1744, Oil on canvas

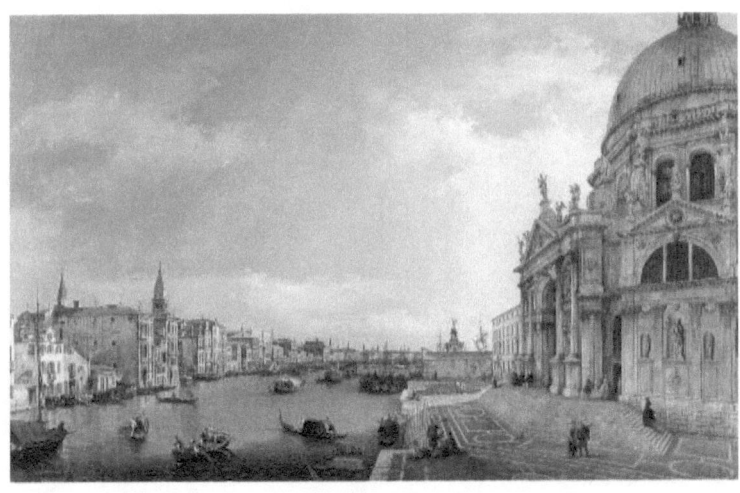

The Grand Canal with S.Maria della Salute towards the
Riva degli Schiavoni, 1744, Oil on canvas

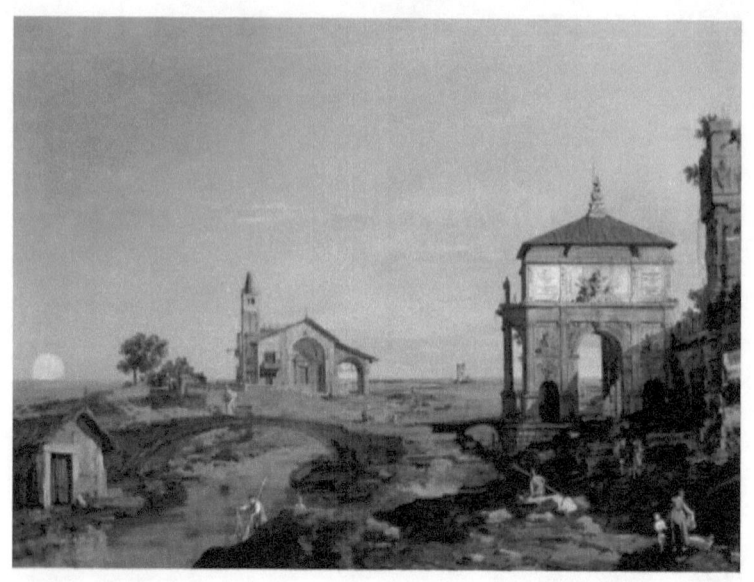

An Island in the Lagoon with a Gateway and a Church,
1744, Oil on canvas

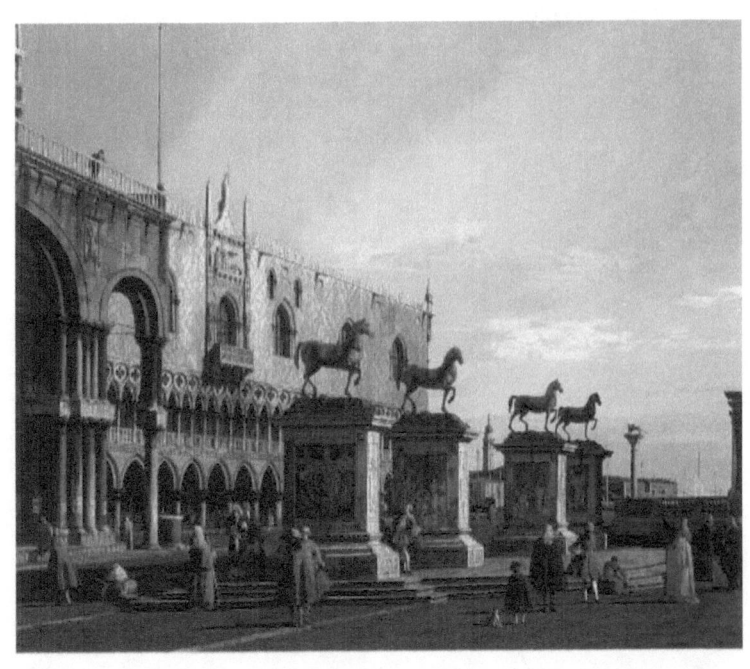

Venice: Capriccio With the Four Horses From the
Cathedral of San Marco, 1744, Oil on canvas

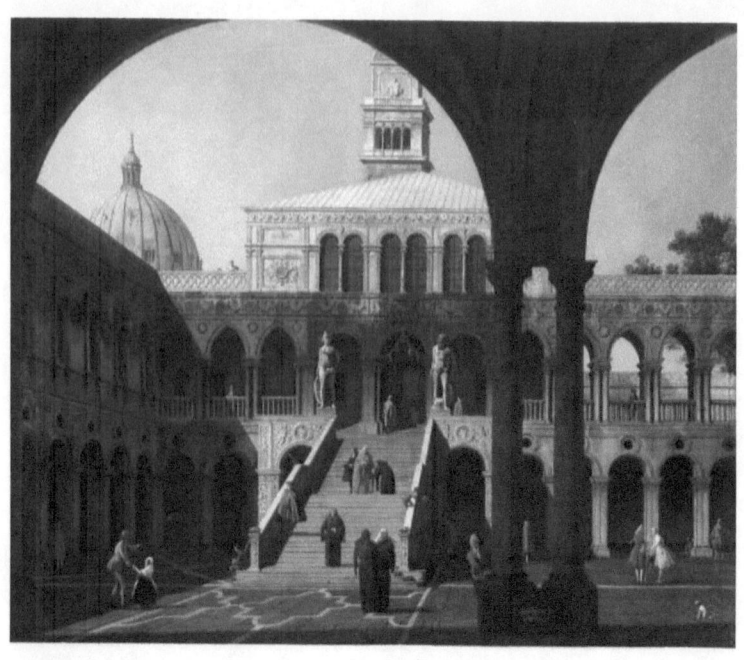

Venice: Caprice View of the Courtyard of the Doge's
Palace with the Scala dei Giganti, 1744, Oil on canvas

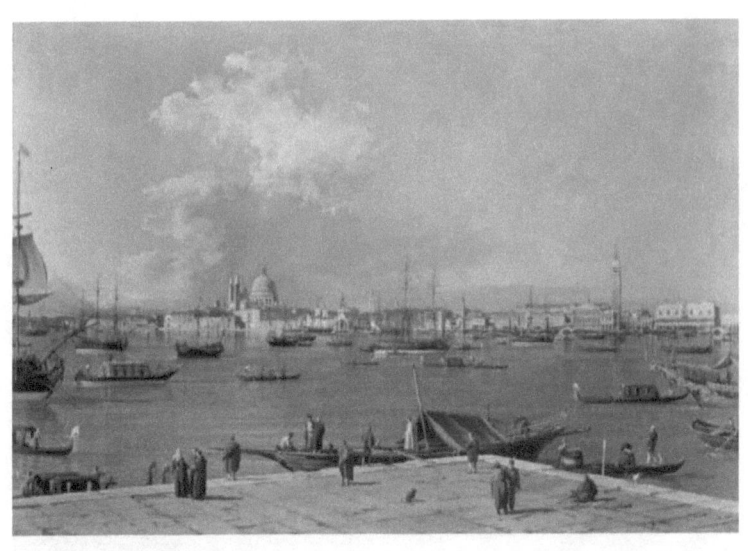

Venice: The Bacino di San Marco from San Giorgio
Maggiorep 1744, Oil on canvas

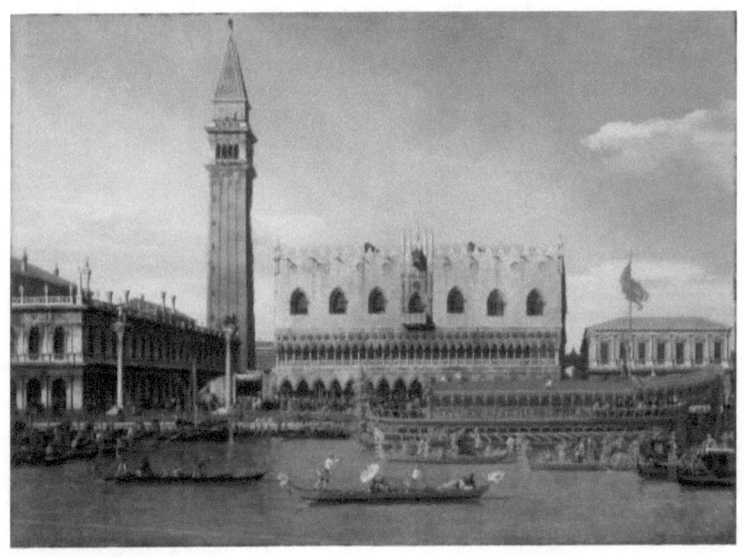

The Bucintoro at the Molo on Ascension Day, 1745
Oil on canvas

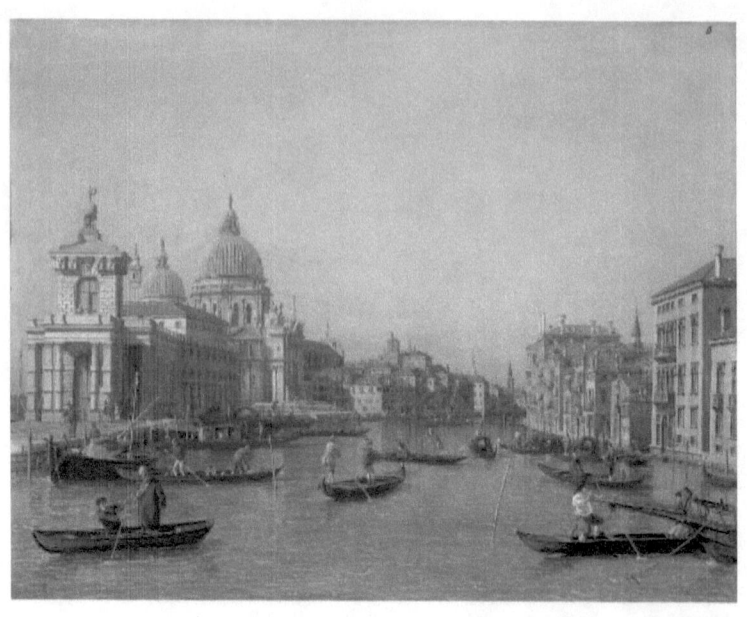

The entrance to the Grand Canal at the Punta della
Dogana and Santa Maria della Salute, 1745
Oil on canvas

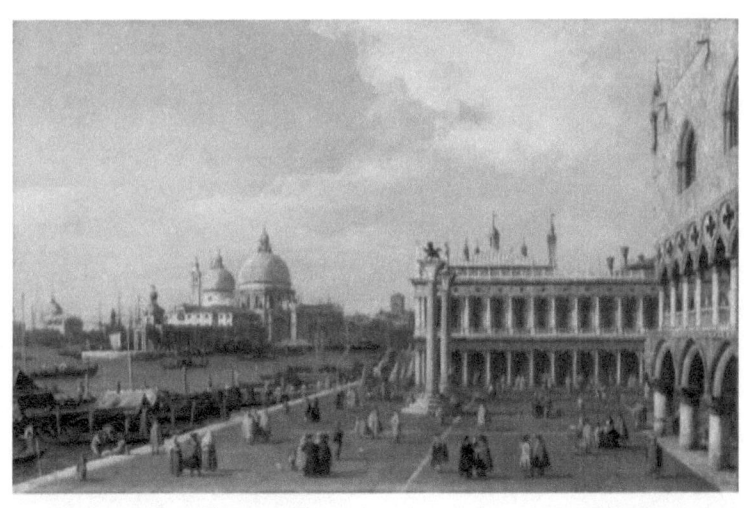

The Mole with Santa Maria della Salute, 1745
Oil on canvas

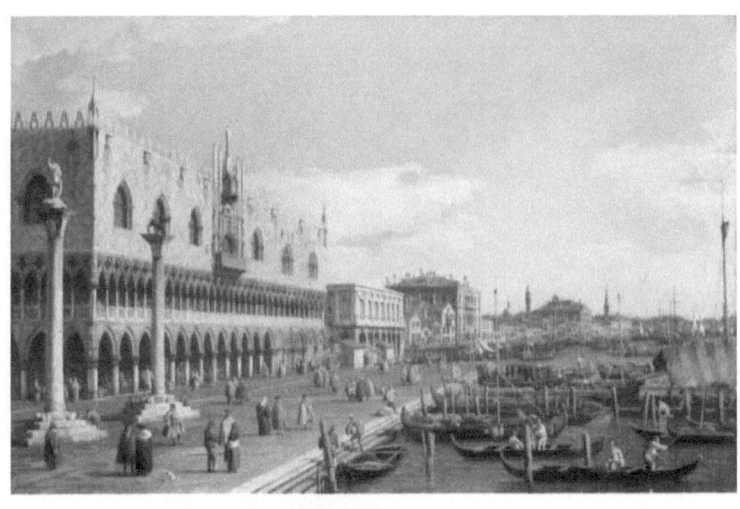

Venice, the Riva degli Schiavoni, 1745
Oil on canvas

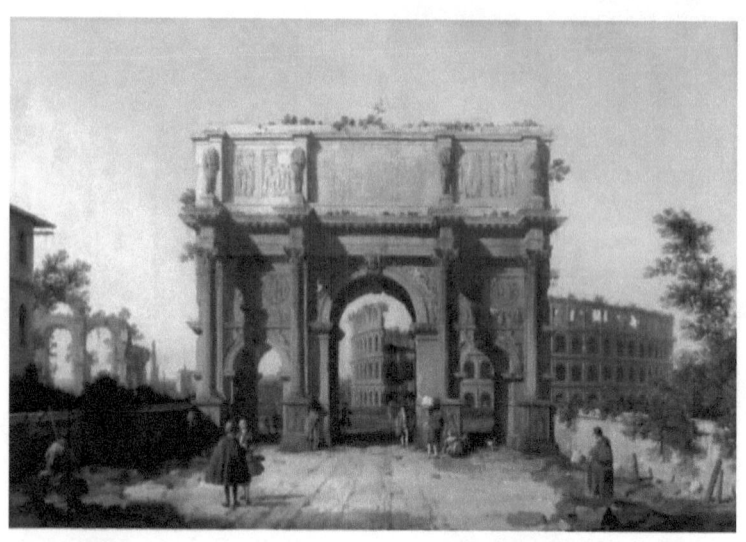

View the Arch of Constantine with the Coliseum, 1745
Oil on canvas

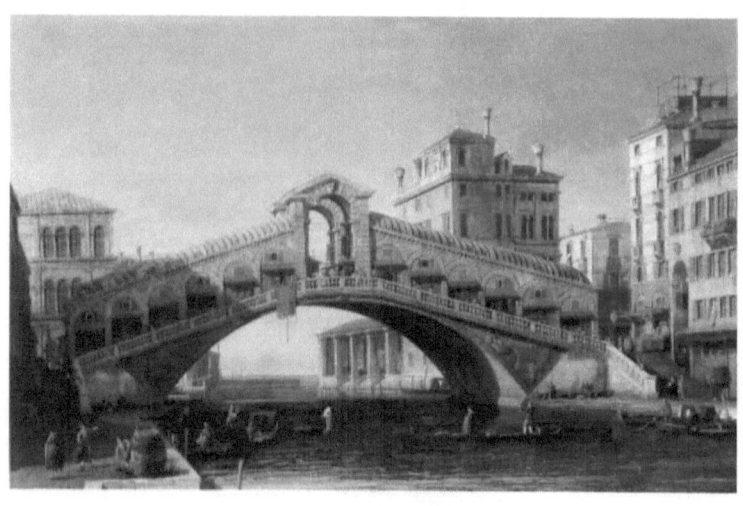

Capriccio of the Rialto Bridge with the Lagoon Beyond,
1746, Oil on canvas

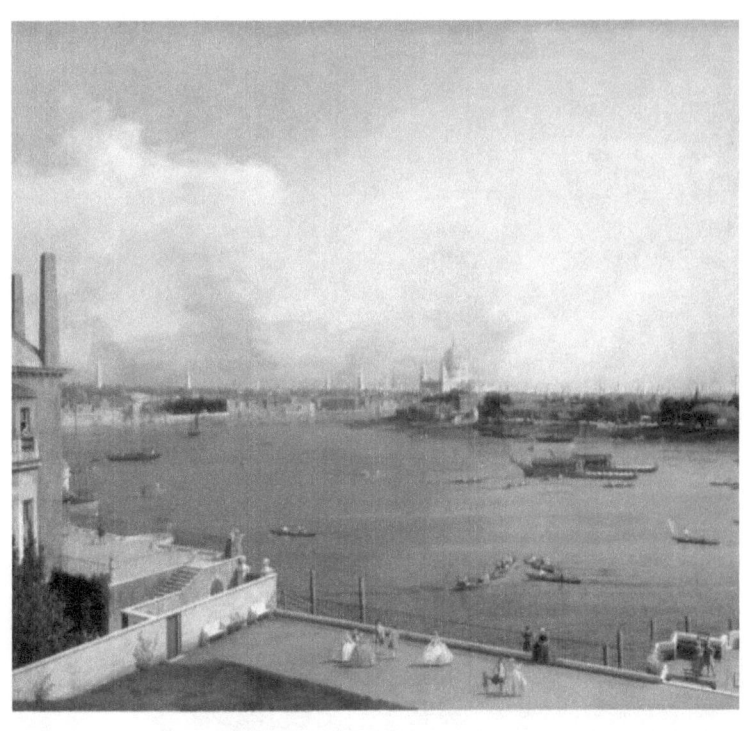

The Thames and the City of London from Richmond
House, 1746
Oil on canvas

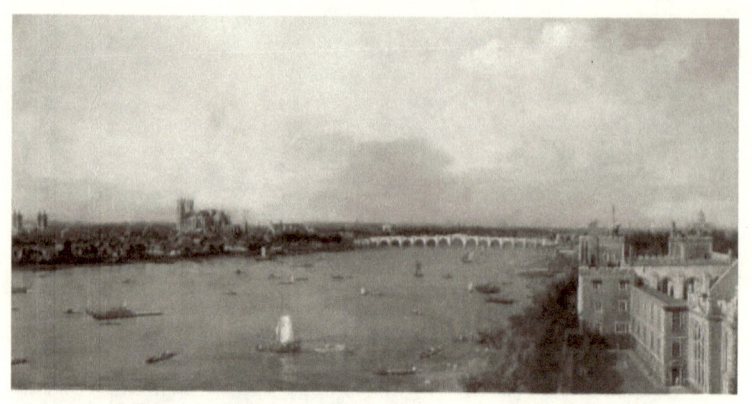

The Thames with St. Paul's Cathedral, 1746
Oil on canvas

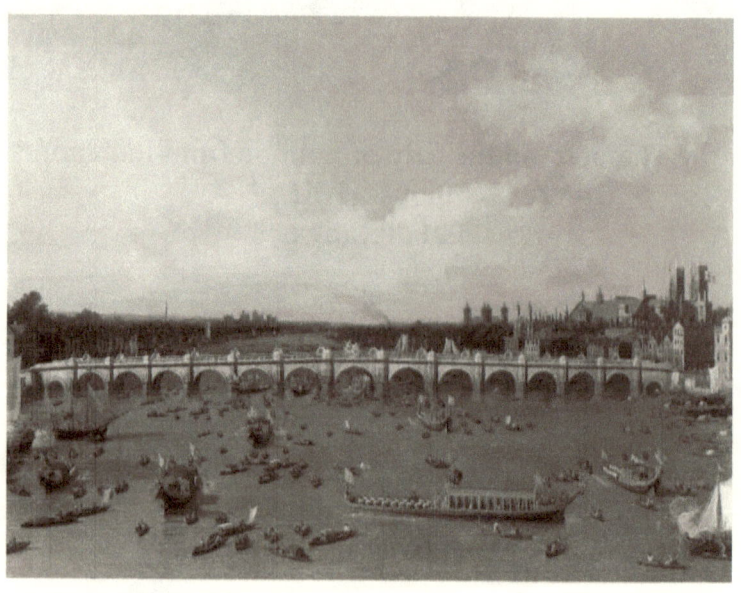

Westminster Bridge from the north on Lord Mayor's
Day, 1746, Oil on canvas

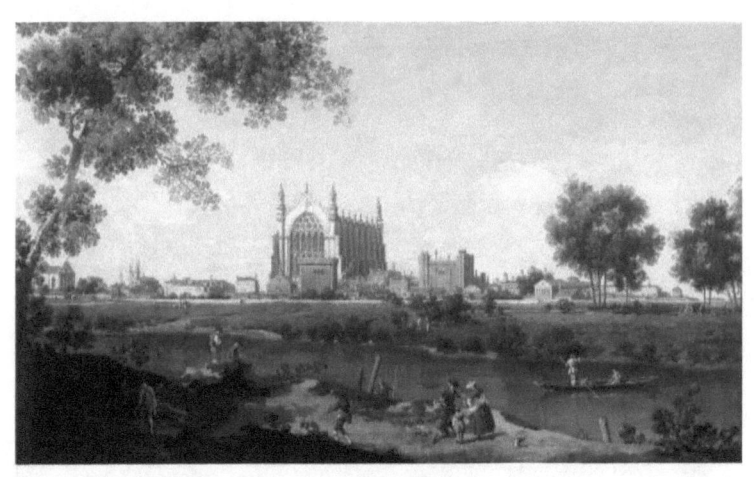

The Chapel of Eton College, 1747
Oil on canvas

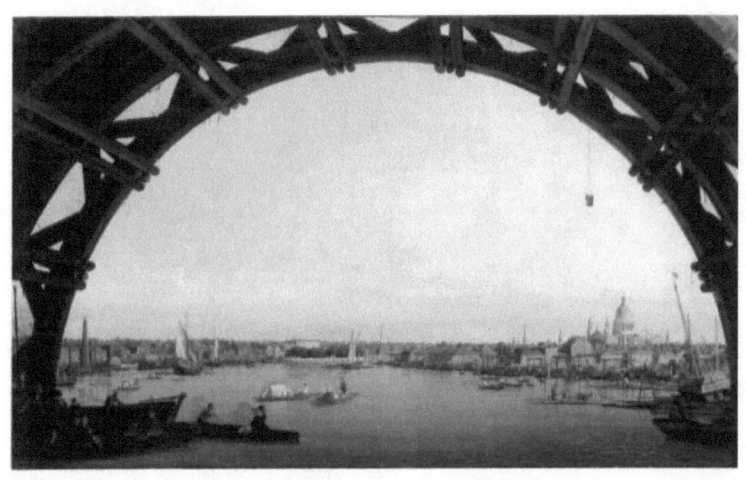

The City Seen Through an Arch of Westminster Bridge,
1747
Oil on canvas

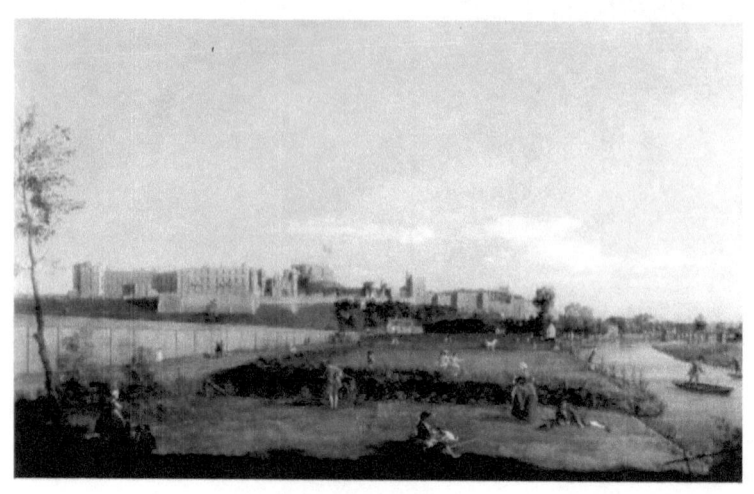

Windsor Castle, 1747
Oil on canvas

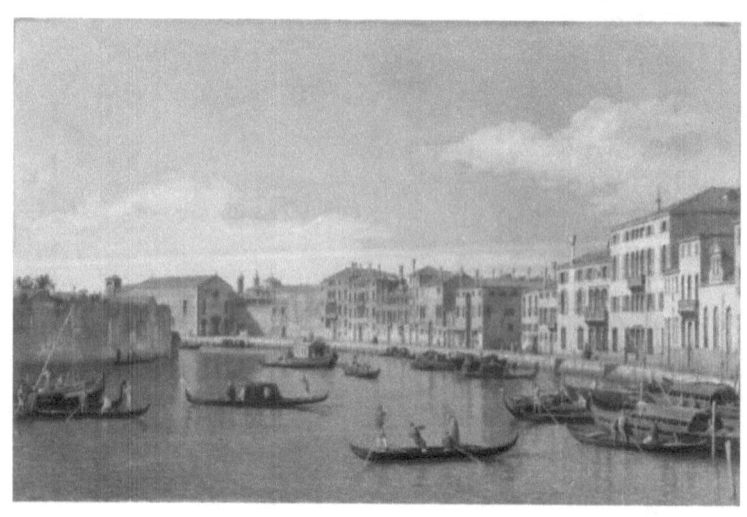

The Canale di Santa Chiari, 1747
Oil on canvas

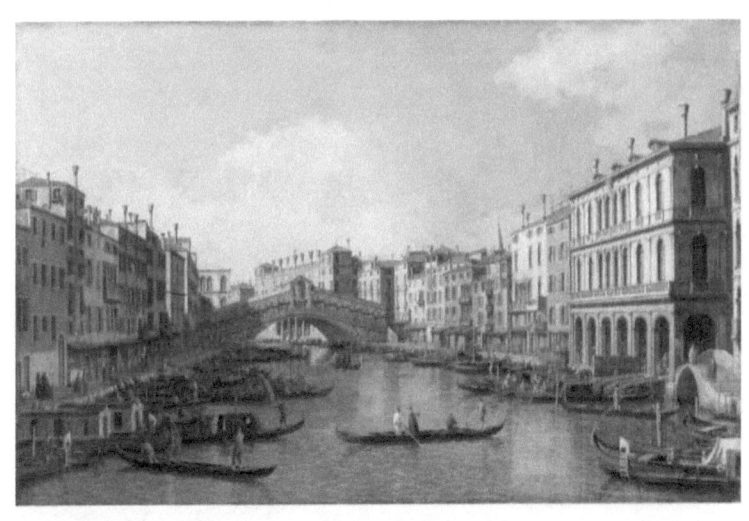

The Grand Canal from the Palazzo Dolfin, 1750
Oil on canvas

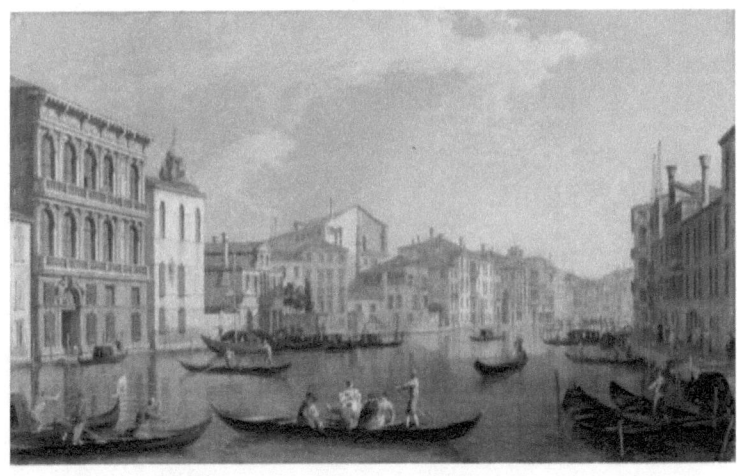

The Grand Canal from the Palazzo Flangini, 1750
Oil on canvas

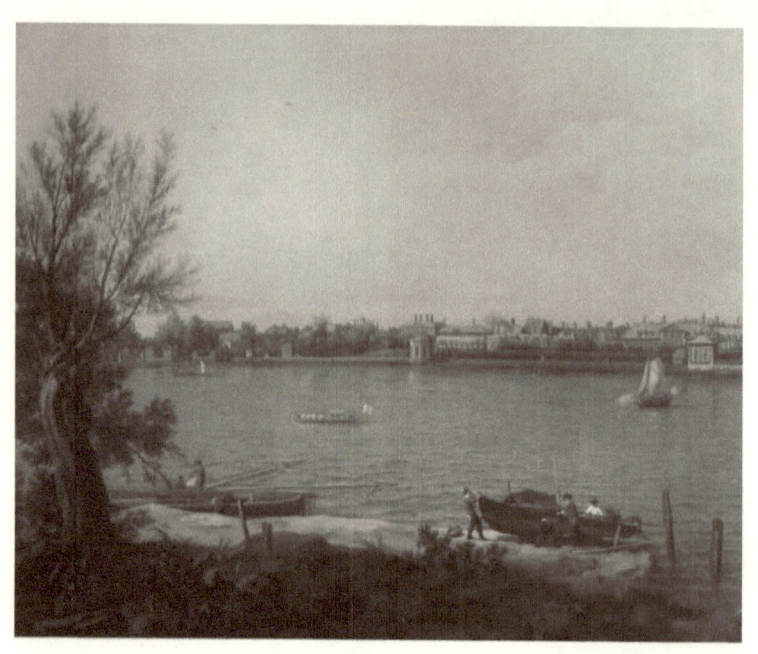

Chelsea from the Thames at Battersea Reach, 1851
Oil on canvas

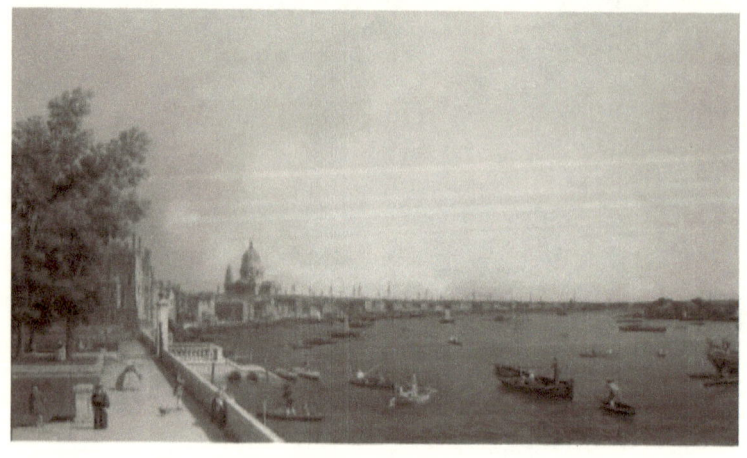

London: The Thames from Somerset House Terrace
towards the Cityp 1751, Oil on canvas

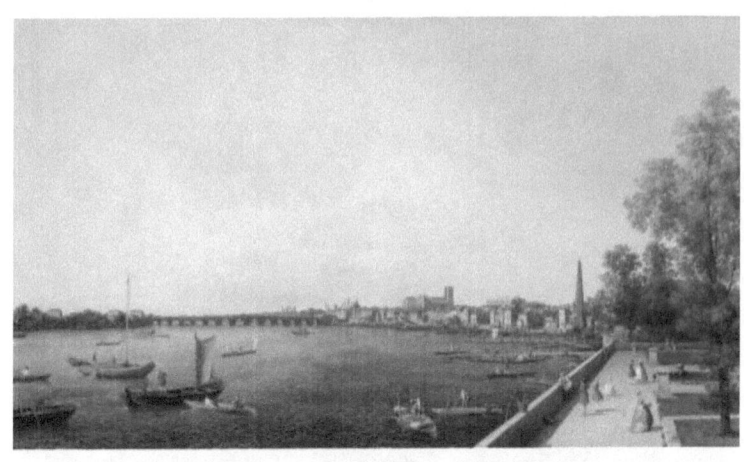

London: The Thames from Somerset House Terrace
towards Westminster, 1751, Oil on canvas

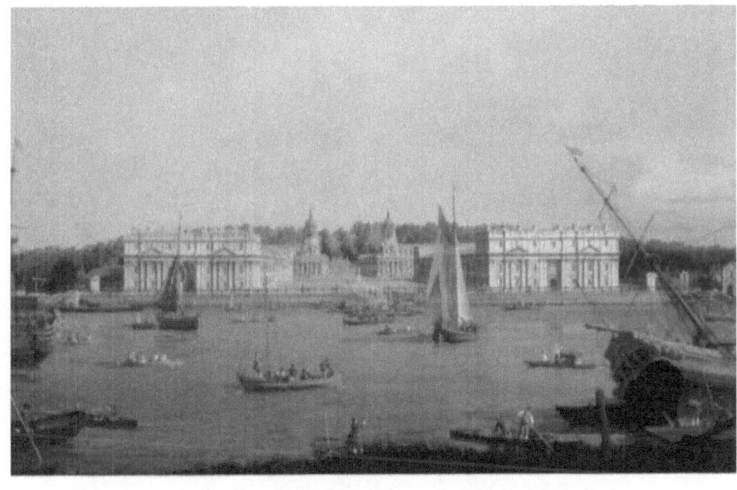

Greenwich Hospital from the North Bank of the
Thames, 1752, Oil on canvas

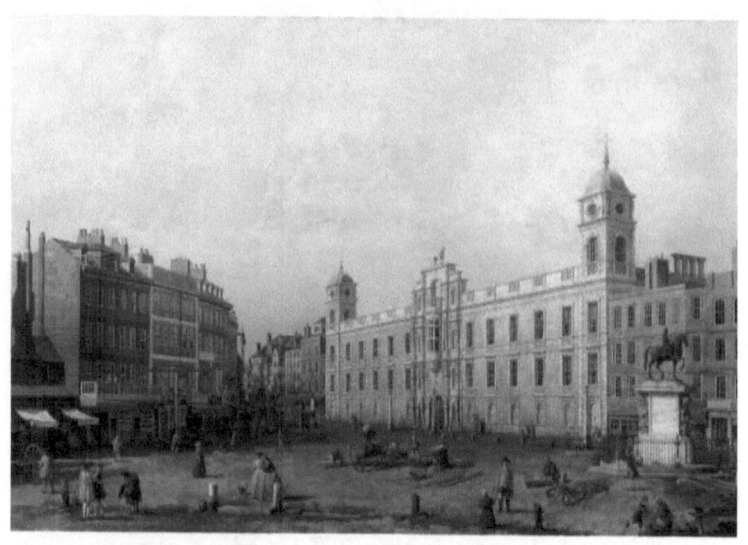

Northumberland House, 1752
Oil on canvas

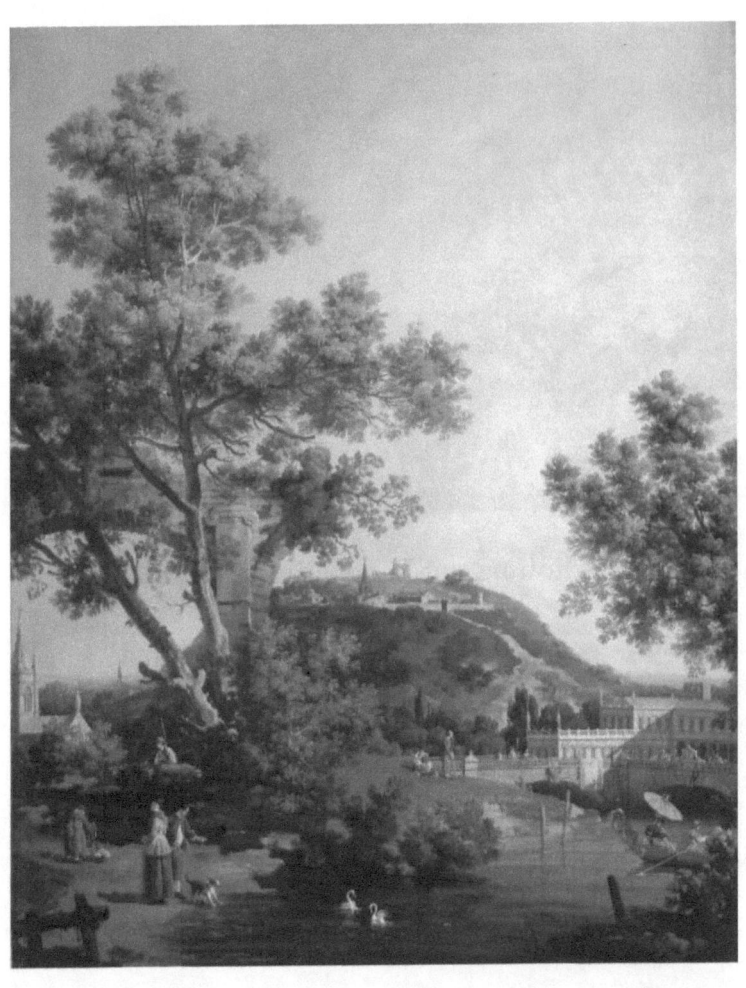

English Landscape Capriccio with a Palace, 1754
Oil on canvas

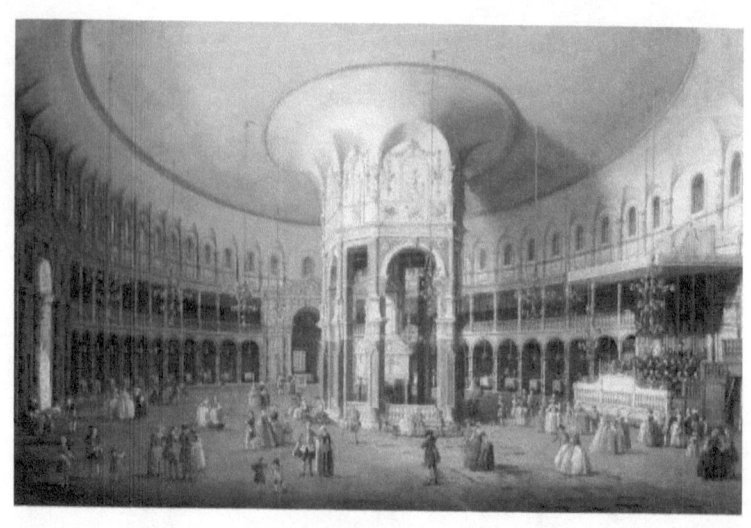

The Rotunda of Ranelagh House, 1754
Oil on canvas

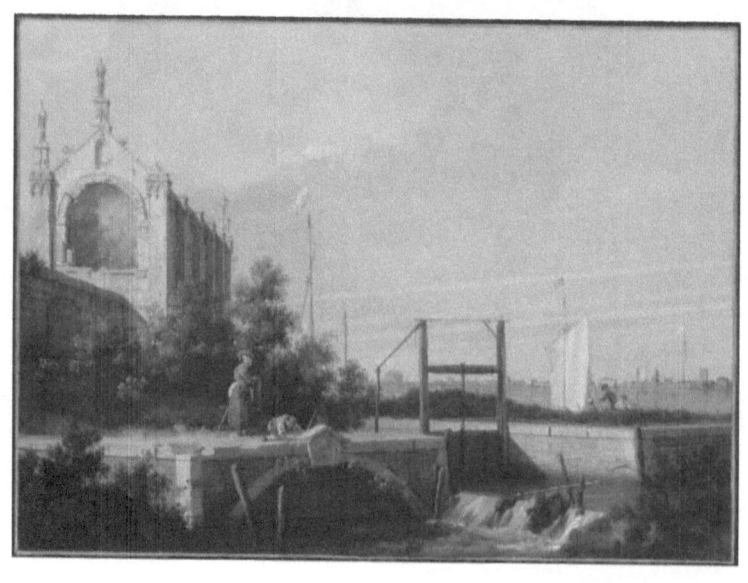

A Sluice on a River with a Chapel, 1754
Oil on canvas

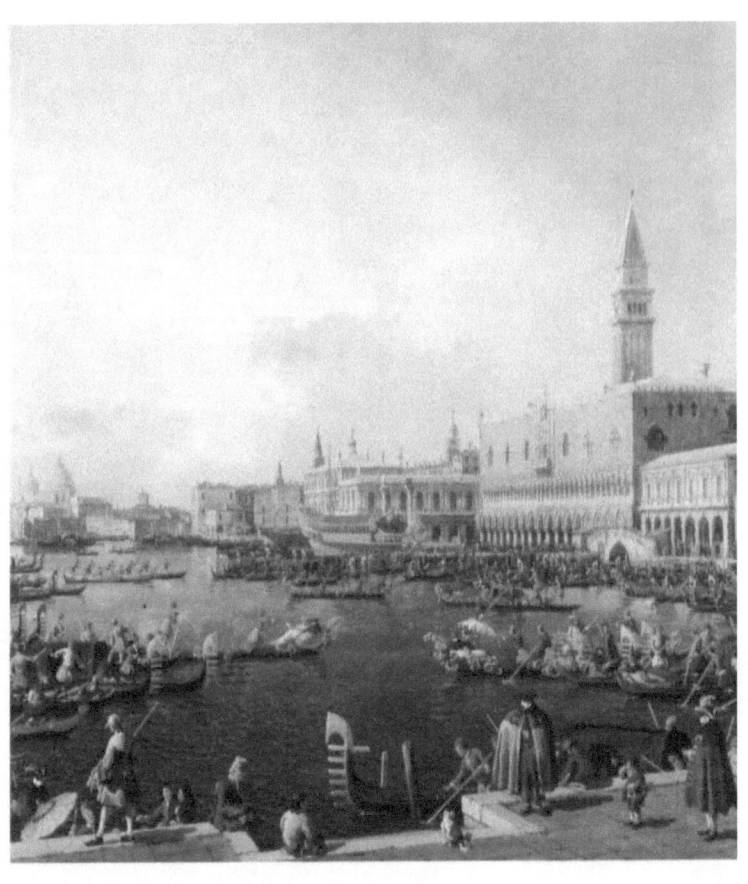

Venice, Bacino di San Marco on Ascension Day, 1754
Oil on canvas

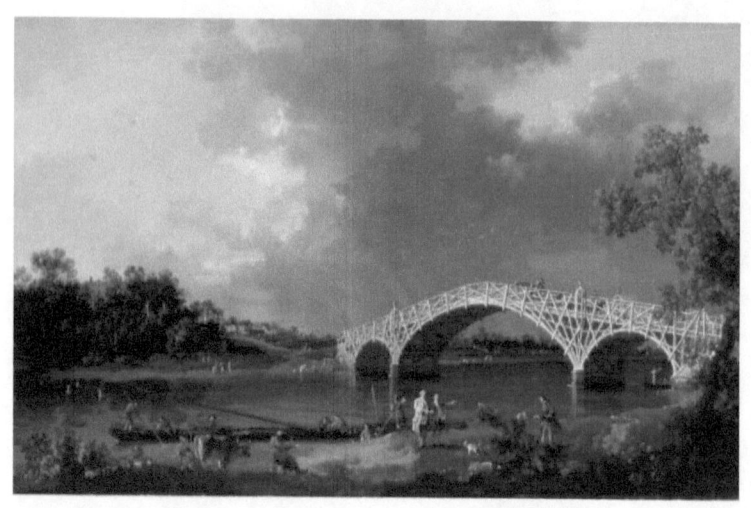

A View of Walton Bridge, 1754
Oil on canvas

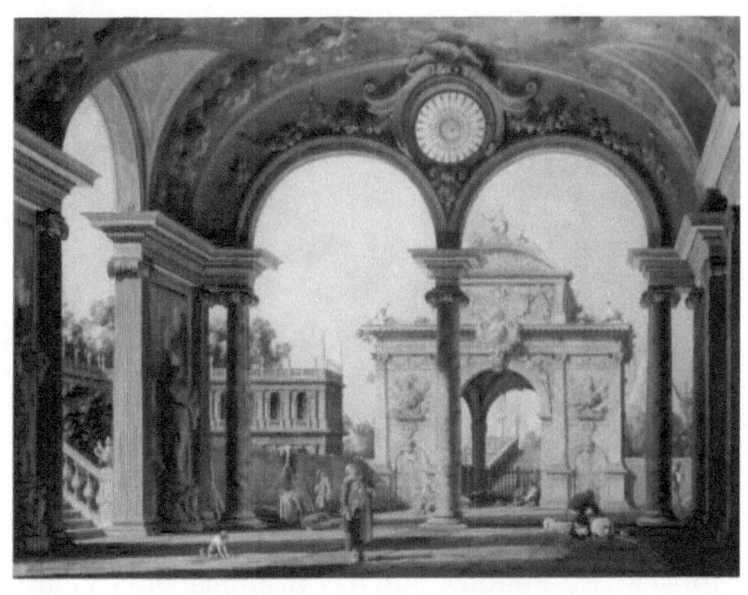

Capriccio of a Renaissance Triumphal Arch seen from
the Portico of a Palace, 1755, Oil on canvas

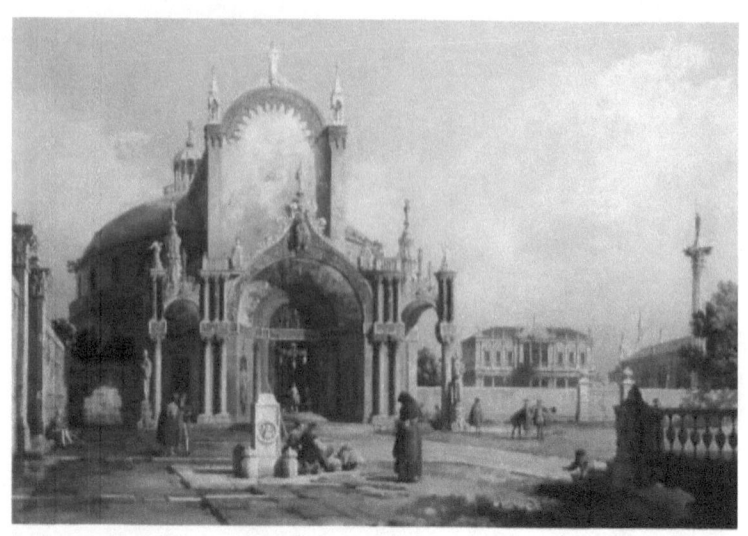

Capriccio of a Round Church with an Elaborate Gothic
Portico in a Piazza, a Palladian Piazza and a Gothic
Church Beyond, 1755, Oil on canvas

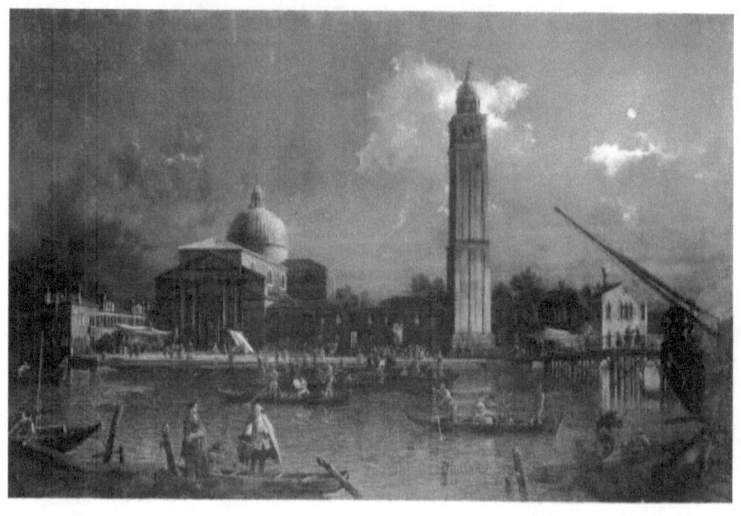

Night-time Celebration Outside the Church of San
Pietro di Castello, 1755, Oil on canvas

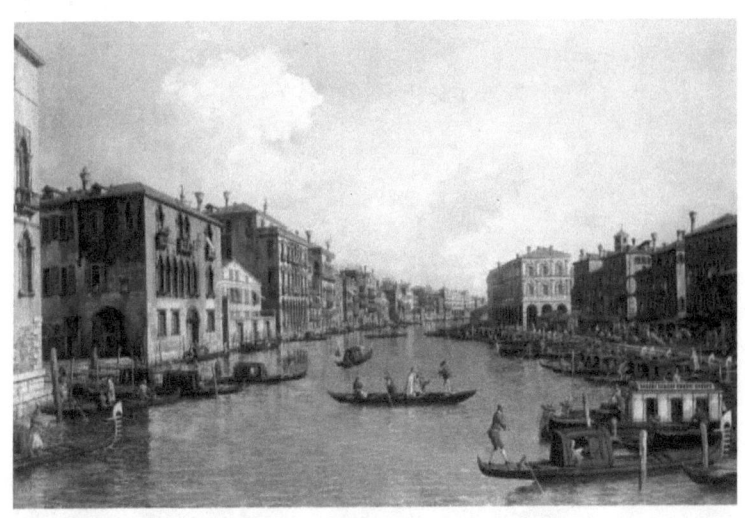

Grand Canal from the Campo Santa Sofia towards the
Rialto Bridge, 1756
Oil on canvas

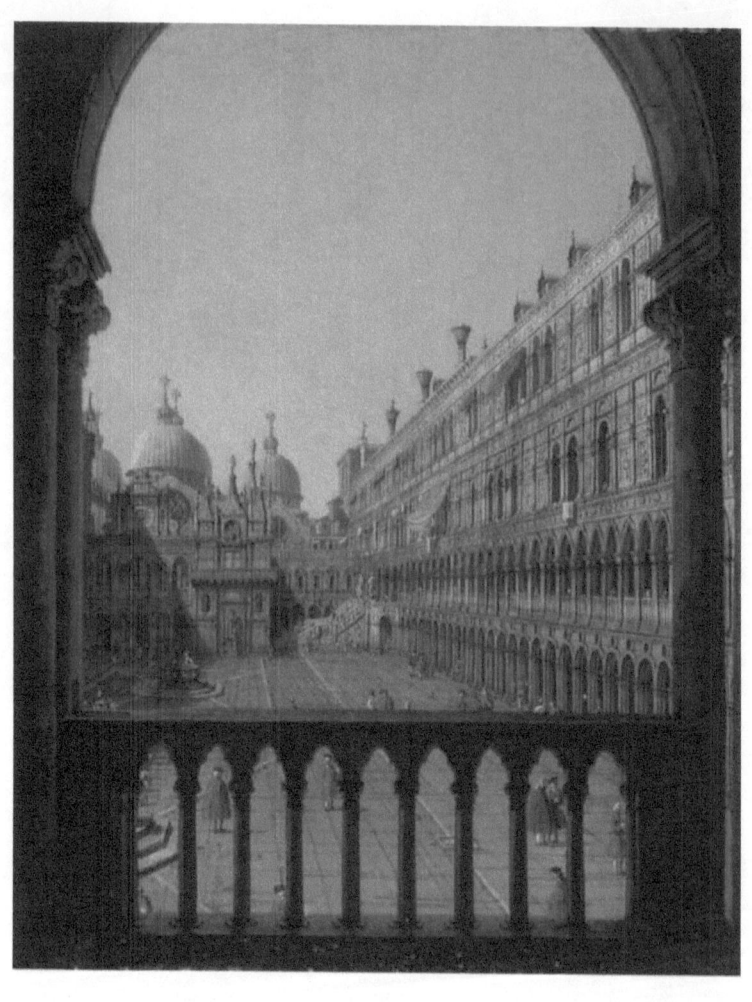

Interior Court of the Doge's Palace, Venice, 1756
Oil on canvas

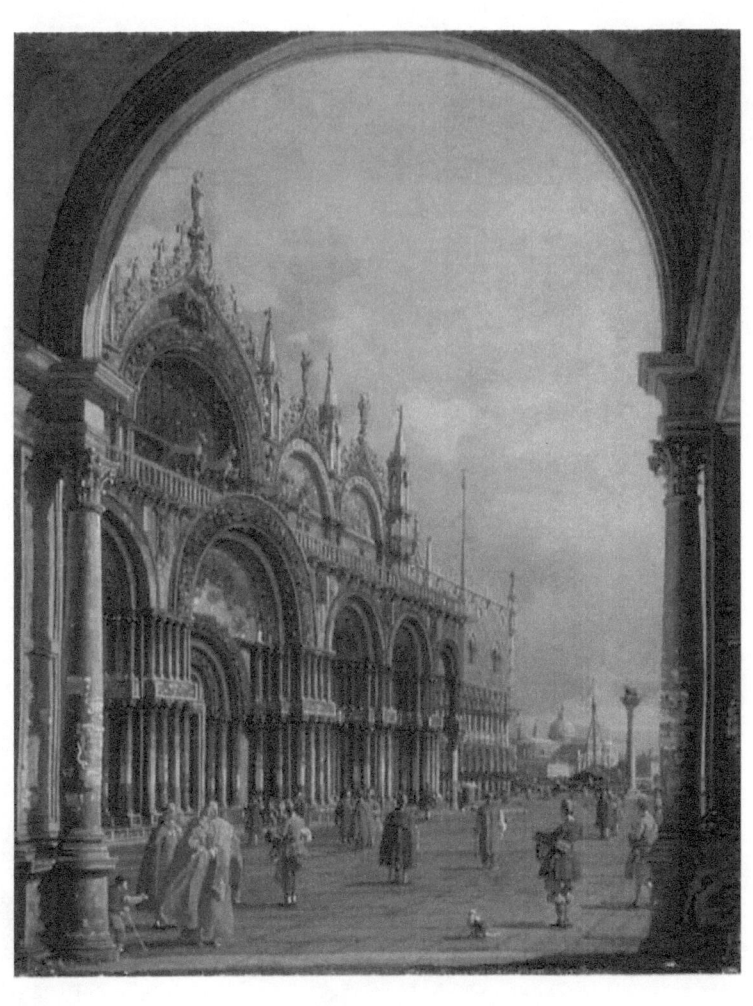

St Mark's, Venice, 1756
Oil on canvas

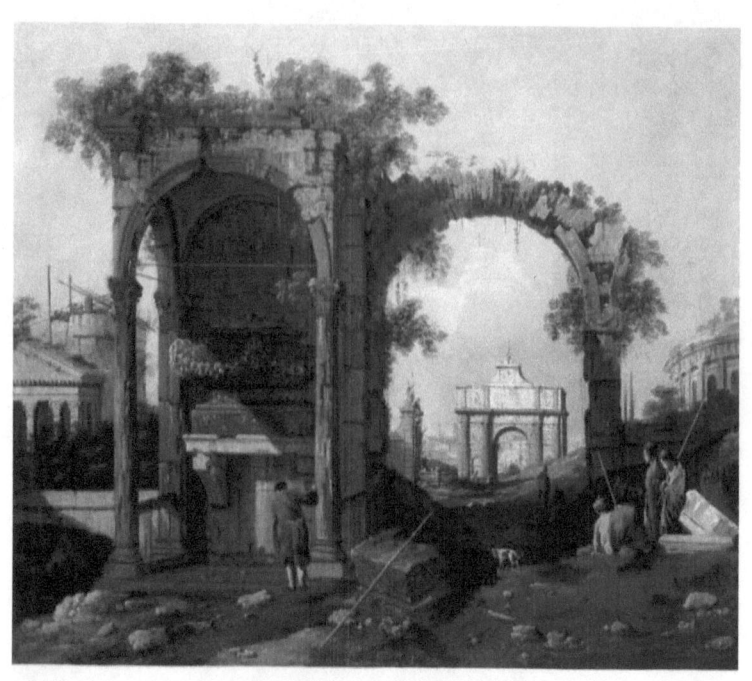

Landscape with Ruins, 1759
Oil on canvas

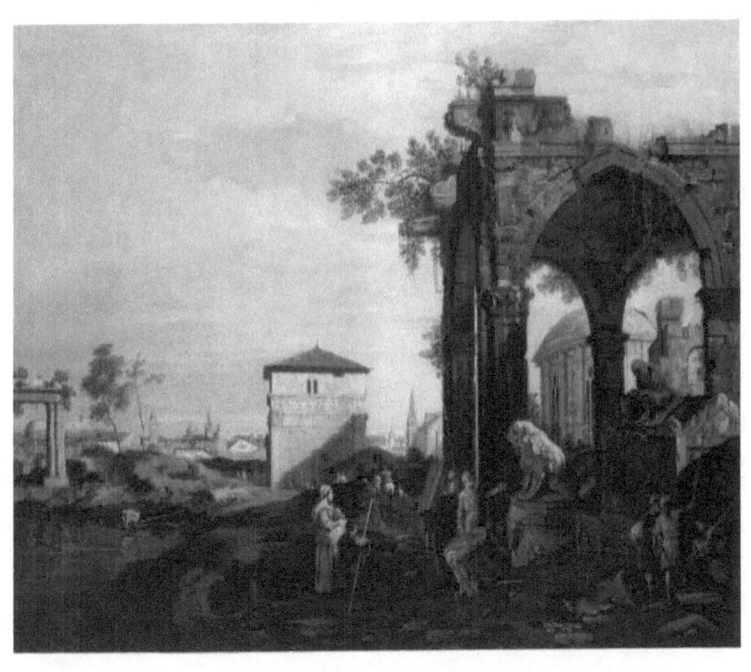

Landscape with Ruins, 1759
Oil on canvas

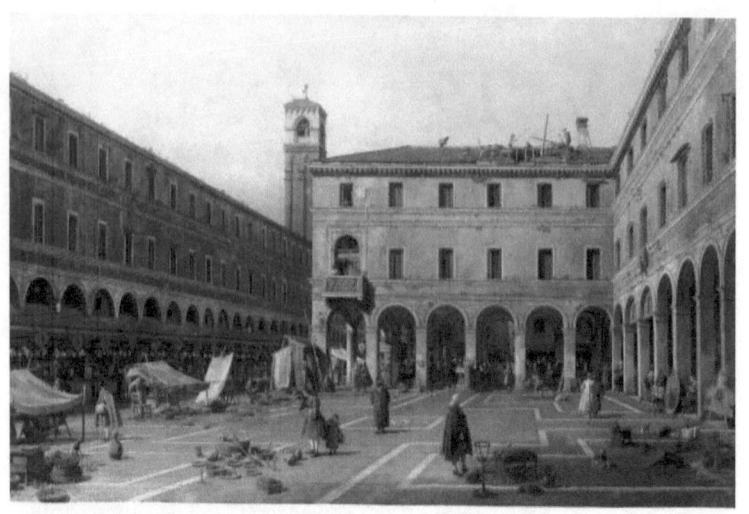

Campo di Rialto, 1760
Oil on canvas

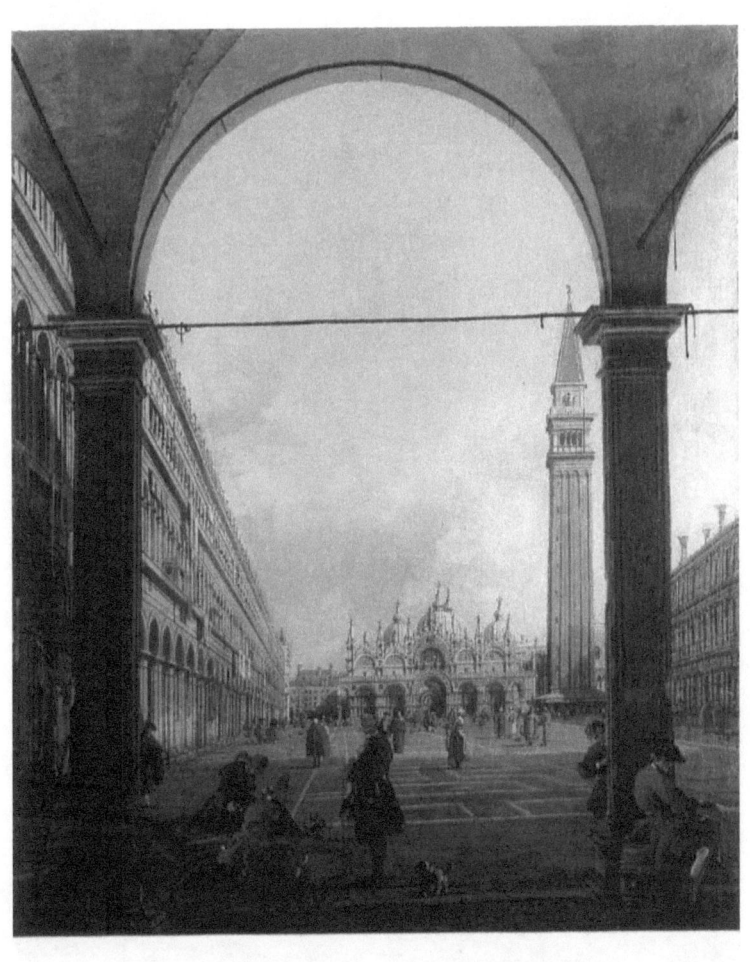

Piazza San Marco, Looking East, 1760
Oil on canvas

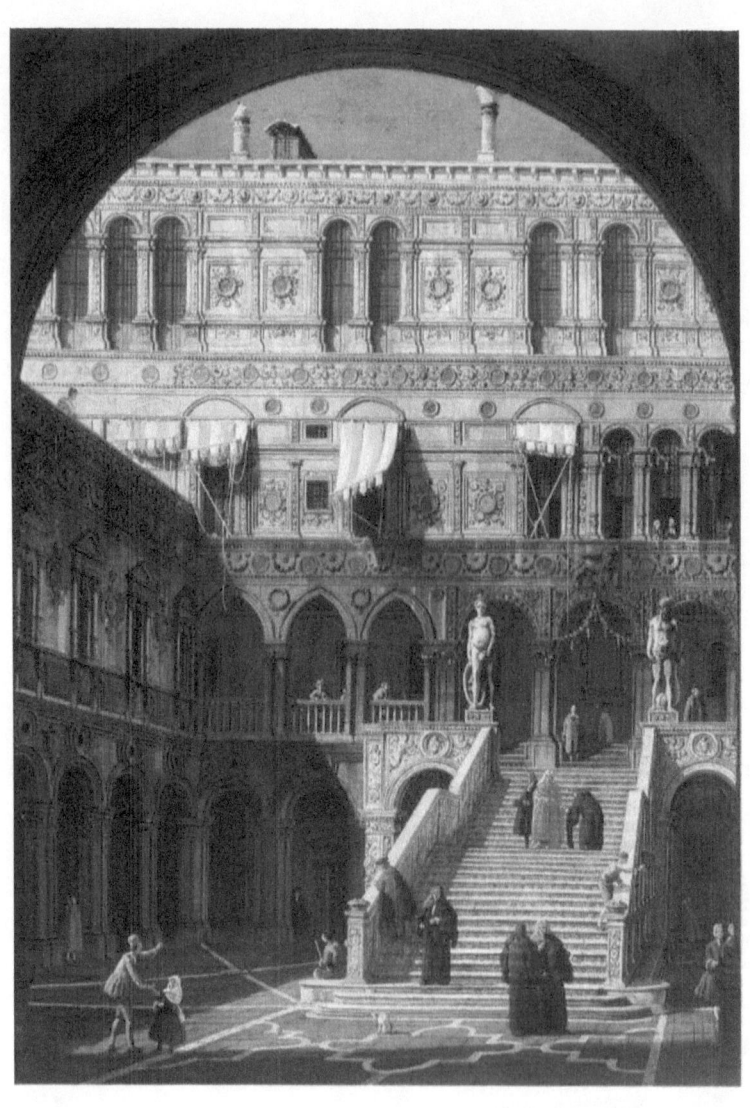

Scala dei Giganti, 1765
Oil on canvas

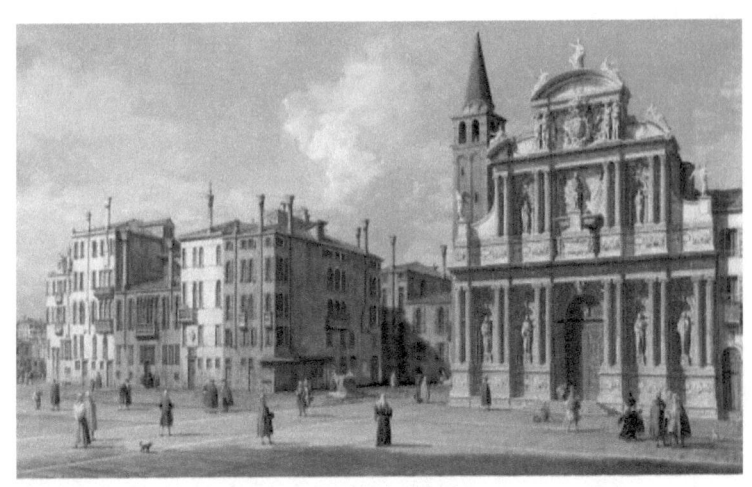

Santa Maria Zobenigo, 1769
Oil on canvas

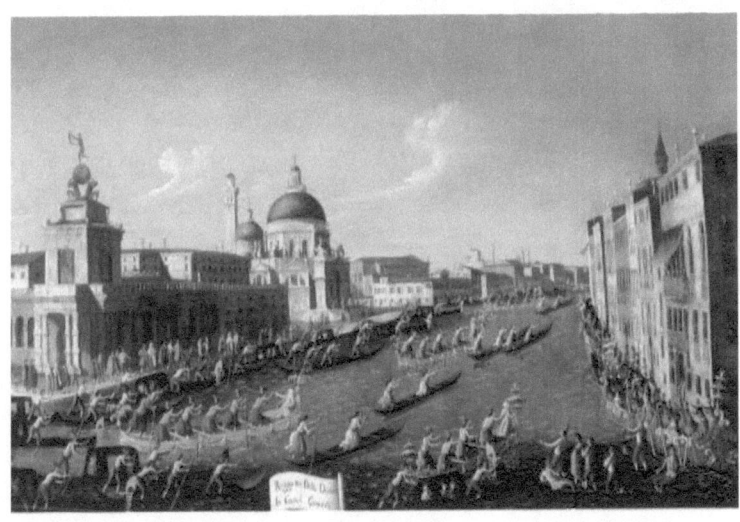

The Women's Regatta on the Grand Canal, 1769
Oil on canvas

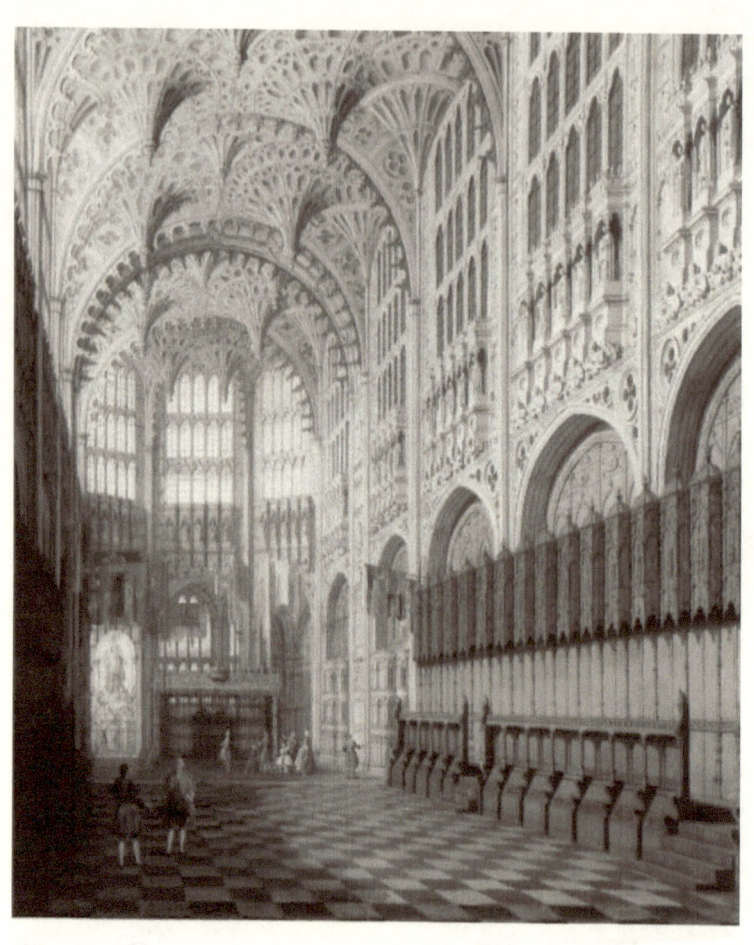

The Interior of Henry VII's Chapel in Westminster
Abbey
Oil on canvas

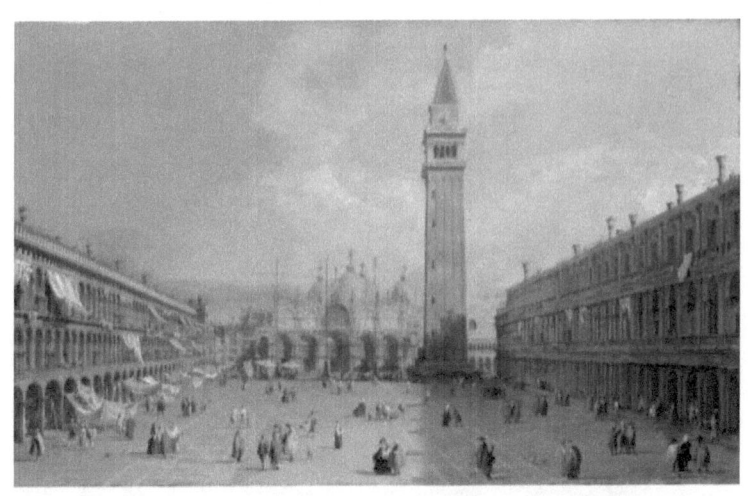

Piazza San Marco
Oil on canvas

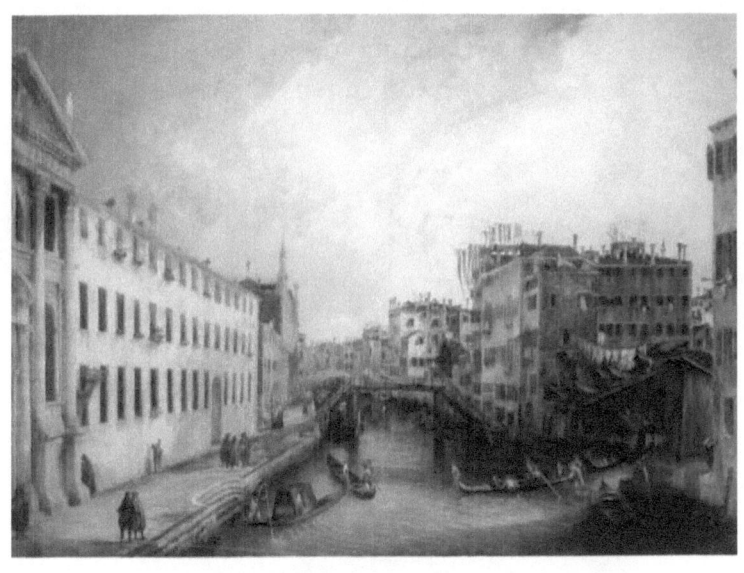

Rio dei Mendicanti: Looking South
Oil on canvas

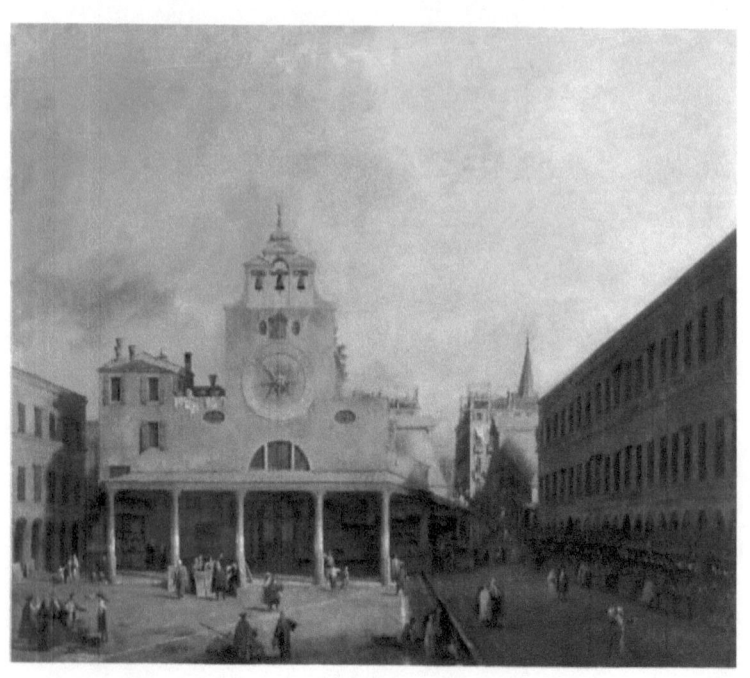

San Giacomo de Rialto
Oil on canvas

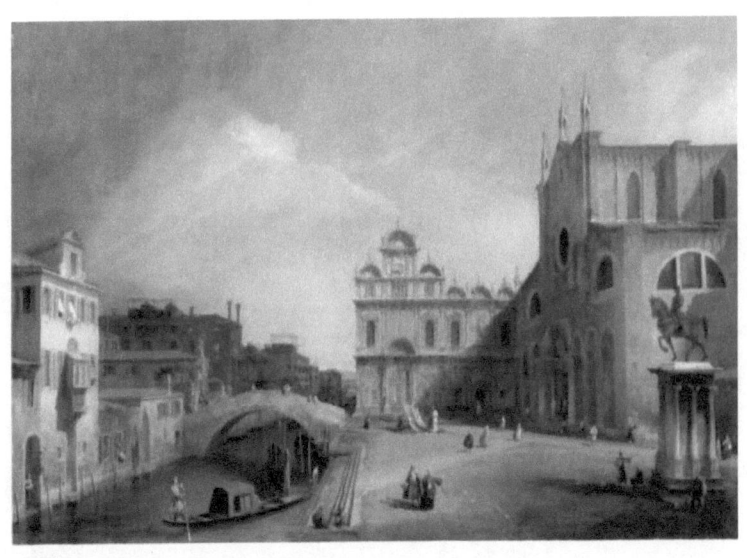

Santi Giovanni e Paolo and the Scuola di San Marco
Oil on canvas

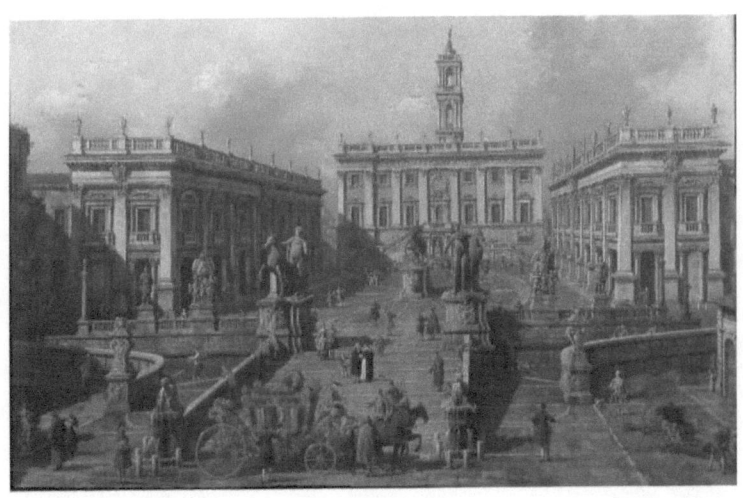

View of Rome The Piazza del Campidoglio and the
Cordonata, Oil on canvas

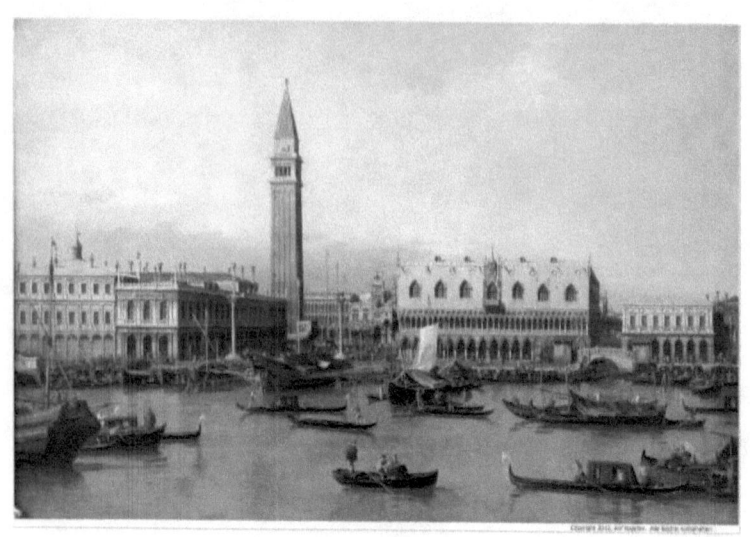

View of the Doge's Palace in Venice
Oil on canvas

www.ingramcontent.com/pod-product-compliance
Lightning Source LLC
Chambersburg PA
CBHW020929180526
45163CB00007B/2939

* 9 7 8 1 5 0 5 8 7 2 1 0 1 *